TEEN ESTEEM

Hello Alec,

We met once on vacation, both our families were in Old Saybrook, Conn. Your dad is a fantastic person. If you grow up and have his personality and professional ethic, you will turn out just fine!

So, this book has been really my family... I hope it helps and you enjoy reading it alone & w. others in your family.

Hope to see you another time!

Best wishes,
Nancy Zucker

TEEN ESTEEM

Parents, friends, siblings & YOU

Sarah Chana Radcliffe

First published 1992

Copyright © 1992 by Sarah Chana Radcliffe
ISBN 0-944070-80-9

All rights reserved

No part of this publication may be translated, reproduced, stored in a retrieval system or transmitted, in any form or by any means, electronic, mechanical, photocopying, recording or otherwise, without prior permission in writing from both the copyright holder and the publisher.

Phototypeset at Targum Press

Published by:
Targum Press Inc.
22700 W. Eleven Mile Rd.
Southfield, Mich. 48034

Distributed by:
Feldheim Publishers
200 Airport Executive Park
Spring Valley, N.Y. 10977

Distributed in Israel by:
Nof Books Ltd.
POB 23646
Jerusalem 91235

Printed in Israel

In loving memory of our mother and grandmother,
Fanny Krieger, ע"ה
פייגיל חיה בתביילא דינה
a source of strength and joy to us always.

Acknowledgments

Many, many thanks to Malky Edery, Suffy Friedberg, Lauren and Jarod Bensky, Brenna Leah Radcliffe, and all of the other wonderful teenage readers who read the manuscript and offered valuable feedback. Thanks, too, to the students of Bais Yaakov of Toronto, who took the time to describe the issues that were important to them.

I also want to thank the lady in New York (and her daughters) who inspired this book.

Thanks once more to Rabbi Moshe Englander, principal of the Mesivta of Toronto, for checking the halachic accuracy of the text.

Table of Contents

	Preface 9	
1	**Understanding Yourself** 13	
	The Bad Judge 16	
	Self-Esteem 20	
	Positive Power 24	
	Changing Tapes 26	
	Positive Power Tapes 32	
	"I'm Intelligent." 32	
	"I'm an Important and Valuable Person." 35	
	"My Body Is Fine the Way It Is." 38	
	"I Am Entitled to Make Mistakes and Benefit from Them." 40	
	"I'm a Successful Person." 43	
	"I'm Okay the Way I Am." 47	
	"I Am Loveable." 51	
	"I Am Allowed to Have My Feelings." 53	
	"I Can Take Care of Myself." 57	
	"I Can Make a Decision." 61	

2	**Understanding Parents** **67**
	When Parents Criticize 72
	When Parents Seem to Make
	Excessive Demands 79
	When Parents Limit You 81
	When Parents Don't Understand You 86
	Getting Along With Parents 90
	Instead of Headaches 93

3	**Understanding Siblings** **98**
	Say It With Words 101
	Use a Normal Tone of Voice 103
	Don't Label or Name-Call 105
	Accept Complaints Graciously 107
	Give In 110
	Do Things for Your Siblings 112
	Say Nice Things 114
	Share Possessions 115
	Respect the Property of Your Siblings 118
	Share Space 120
	Refuse to Fight 122
	Treat Siblings the Way You Want
	to Be Treated 124

4	**Understanding Friends** **127**
	Being a Friend 130
	Create a Pleasant First Impression 131
	Realize You Have Something to Offer 132
	Be a Good Listener 134
	Be Assertive 141
	Develop Qualities of a Good Friend 149

5	**Being Happy**	157
	Look for the Good	159
	Watch Your Language	162
	Pursue Serenity	164
	Avoid Anger	168
	Manage Your Moods	172
	Be a Problem-Solver	174
	Set Your Own Standards	178
	Throw Yourself Into Life	180
6	**Caring: The Key to Success**	183
	Notes	191

Preface

Leah was positively beaming. Today, she knew, was going to be a terrific day — like yesterday and the day before. Not that everything was going to be perfect (she knew she couldn't control the world, after all), but she also knew that she was equipped to handle whatever came her way — not only the great things but also the challenges and problems. You name it, she could manage it beautifully. And more than that, she knew how to make the best of every situation and really enjoy it! Leah was packed full of fantastic life-skills, skills which would see her over every hurdle, skills which would bring joy and happiness into every hour of her life. Where did Leah get these incredible skills? She read Teen Esteem*!*

Teen Esteem is a success manual for people of all ages and all situations. The examples are about young people, but the ideas apply equally to everyone up to and including senior citizens! Parents can read the book and apply the skills to their own lives; they can bring it to the dinner table for family discussion; they can use it to understand their growing children. Teenagers and young adults can read it on their own, selecting chapters and issues that they're most interested in or reading it through thoroughly for a deeper understanding of human psychology. They can use it to help themselves and to help their friends and family.

Everyone can benefit from reading *Teen Esteem*: people who live happy, uncomplicated lives, people who face many challenges, people who have lots of self-confidence, and people who have none. *Teen Esteem* takes you on a journey of human relationships; it examines your relationship to yourself, to your parents, siblings, and friends. It explains the pitfalls of these relationships, things that can go wrong and how to make them right. It shows you what you can do to affect people around you and it shows you how you are affected by others.

"That's very nice, but I don't need to know all that. I've got a great family, plenty of friends, and all the success I could want."

Even people who are totally satisfied with their lives can benefit from reading *Teen Esteem*. After all, nobody is perfect. And if you're self-confident and happy, you'd probably like to be able to help others achieve your level of success. *Teen Esteem* will give you a rare insight into the dynamics of personality, what makes people tick. With that knowledge you can help to bring out the best in others — and in yourself, too.

Preface 11

Moreover, *Teen Esteem* is fun reading. You'll meet lots of people with interesting life-situations and dilemmas. You'll get a glimpse into their minds and hearts. Although all of these people are fictitious, they represent the broad spectrum of real-life people and real-life challenges. Their experiences are based on the experiences of people like yourself and those you know, so you'll easily identify with their concerns.

Teen Esteem is, above all, real. And it gives you authentic Jewish strategies for coping successfully with issues that are important in your life. Read, learn, and enjoy!

1
Understanding Yourself

WHO ARE YOU? Look at this list of words and circle the ones that you would use to describe yourself:

smart	kind	lazy
bad	careless	enthusiastic
good looking	plain	boring
shy	exciting	friendly
determined	brave	worried
sad	ugly	pessimistic
ambitious	giving	funny
good	selfish	curious
optimistic	messy	energetic
cooperative	creative	talented
cute	angry	disorganized
caring	confident	neat
relaxed	cheerful	nervous
calm	moody	argumentative
helpful	forgetful	responsible
independent		

This list represents only a few of the many possible ways to describe people. There may be words that describe you that are not printed on this list. Take a moment now to add some words that describe your personality — just write them down at the bottom of the list on the previous page.

Good. Now let's discuss the meaning of "personality." Every person has a personality. It is his or her general way of responding to life. The words you circled and wrote above may describe aspects of your personality — your typical ways of behaving and feeling. For example, if you circled the word "confident" it probably means that you feel confident a lot of the time. It's one of your typical ways of feeling. Nonetheless, there are times when you have not felt confident in your life, times when you have felt just the opposite in fact! In addition, even though you generally feel confident, there may be specific situations that make you lack confidence (like hiking along a narrow path on the edge of a cliff!).

Indeed, every person can say that each of the words in the list applies to him at some point in time. Who has never been argumentative? Who has never felt bad, sad, or good? Who has never been careless, shy, or helpful? However, we don't describe ourselves with these words unless we think that these behaviors are very common with us. The person who is argumentative *a lot*, usually circles that word. The person who feels sad *a lot*, usually circles that word.

Here's how Miriam describes her personality:

"I'm quiet. I don't make friends easily because I don't know what to say to people. When I'm with someone I know really

well, though, I'm different. I'm actually quite funny. I think I'm a good friend — I'd say I was generous and thoughtful and kind. At home they say I'm stubborn and lazy because I don't like to help around the house. At school, the teachers say I'm very smart and serious. I know that I worry a lot and I have a lot of fears. I'm afraid of elevators and flying on airplanes, for example. I like drawing and all sorts of crafts like rug hooking and needlepoint. I have the patience for all of that stuff. On the other hand, I have very little patience for some of my brothers and sisters and I often fight with them."

Notice that Miriam has many different aspects to her personality. Depending on who she's with and what situation she's in, she can be shy or outgoing, thoughtful or stubborn, patient or impatient. Personality is not rigid. A shy person is not always shy in every situation. Nor will he always be shy, because personality changes as a person grows and undergoes different experiences. For example, Adam says:

"I used to be very inhibited. I couldn't speak in front of two people — it had to be one-on-one. You'd never believe that now! Now I can sing, dance, speak — you name it — in front of a hundred people at a time! They really encouraged us at yeshivah to acquire these skills, and I can honestly say that if they could turn a guy like me into a public speaker, then they could turn anyone into a public speaker."

So you see, personality can change quite a bit! This, after all, is the basis of being a Jew: our mandate is to continuously change and grow, improving ourselves all the time.

Of course, no one is ever finished growing up. As long as a person is alive, he can (and should!) keep changing and improving. Since every change can bring greater happiness, most people are eager to work on themselves. Who doesn't want to be happier?

The only problem is that we all have an enemy right inside of ourselves that wants to ruin our plans for happiness. Are you surprised to learn that? How else can we explain why we do things that cause us trouble and pain — like arguing with people, criticizing ourselves, worrying about things, getting stuck in bad or sad moods, allowing ourselves to be scared (of tests, public speaking, meeting people, or whatever), not taking care of ourselves, giving up, making excuses, acting helpless, judging others badly, and so on?

Moreover, this "enemy" is a lazy fellow who likes to keep us just the way we are: it's comfortable and easy to stay the same (even if that means being less terrific than we could be), while it can be a little uncomfortable and challenging to change (although the rewards more than compensate for this discomfort).

In addition, this "enemy" gets paid to hang around: there are certain rewards that people get for being sad, mad, scared, or otherwise dysfunctional — rewards like pity, help, or attention from others (positive attention like concern, or even negative attention like advice or complaints). With all that going for it, this enemy is hard to shake.

THE BAD JUDGE

Let's give a name to the enemy within. We'll call it the "Bad Judge." The Bad Judge stunts our growth by making us

Understanding Yourself 17

doubt ourselves and our ability to change. It does this through the mechanism of self-criticism.

Now, this criticism is done in such a sneaky way that you are not even aware that it is happening. This is because the Bad Judge calls itself "I" just as you do. Just as you might say, "I like apple pie," the Bad Judge says, "I am ugly," or "I can't do it." He says these things as if they are statements of fact. From now on, in order to differentiate you from the Bad Judge, we will print the word "I" with a small letter "i" instead of a capital "I" whenever the Bad Judge is speaking. For example, the Bad Judge might say, "i'm so stupid" or "i have no friends."

Where does this Bad Judge come from? It comes from inside your own head in two ways:

1) as a memory of things you were told by people who are important to you, or

2) as conclusions that you made up by yourself.

The Bad Judge speaks to us in a series of messages we'll call "tapes" — because they play over and over again just like tapes in a tape recorder. For example, if a parent often told you that you were selfish, your Bad Judge may repeatedly play a tape inside your head which says, "i'm selfish." In order to turn that tape on, you "push a button." For example, buying a big chocolate bar might be the "button" which reminds you not to share it with anyone because "i am selfish." Similarly, if a parent constantly said, "You're irresponsible," your Bad Judge might say, "i'm irresponsible" when the right button is pushed (e.g., when you're asked to take care of someone's valuable books for a month). If a teacher told you that you'll never be good at math, your Bad Judge may play a tape which says, "i'm not good at math" whenever you're called upon to work with numbers.

Your Bad Judge can also make tapes from your own ideas. For example, if you had difficulty learning to read when you were in first grade, your Bad Judge might make a tape that says, "i'm not a good reader." Nobody had to say it to you; you just drew that conclusion all by yourself. Or, suppose you called two friends to invite them over and both refused to come for various reasons. Your Bad Judge could make the tape, "Nobody likes me. i have no friends."

Once a tape is made, it plays automatically whenever the right button is pushed. For example, if you decide you're not a good reader, then when the button is pushed (by being called upon to read in class), your Bad Judge tape will automatically play: "i'm not a good reader." Normally, the volume of the tape is so quiet that you are not even aware of it playing. Nonetheless, your inner mind hears it loud and clear, and directs you to respond accordingly. That is, one who "is not a good reader" is supposed to panic upon seeing words to read, stumble over them, not be able to think, not enjoy the experience of reading, and not be able to understand what he reads. You will do all of this because that is what your brain will tell you to do in response to the message it receives from your Bad Judge. Bad Judge tapes direct our behavior.

Here is an example of a girl who has a very strong Bad Judge in her head. Her name is Rena.

"i'm so ugly. My hair is frizzy — it makes me look so weird. My boring brown eyes don't even work properly; i need to wear these terrible, speckled glasses. i'm much too skinny — my bones stick out. My nose is too big and my lips are

forever chapped. And to top it all off, my face is dotted with pimples!"

Now, you might say that Rena is just being realistic. After all, if she really has frizzy hair, plain brown eyes, speckled glasses, a big nose, chapped lips, pimples and protruding bones — well, then she is pretty ugly! However, the proof that this is just Rena's Bad Judge speaking is this: about one percent of all people are unusually beautiful, about one percent are actually deformed in a way that would make them ugly, and the remaining ninety-eight per cent are average-looking, with some features that are attractive and some that are plain.

Of these ninety-eight per cent, some people will feel that they are quite attractive and some will feel that they are quite unattractive. Those that listen to their Bad Judge say they're unattractive for any of the following reasons: They could be ignoring their good features and just looking at their plain ones. They could be comparing themselves to professional models or unusually beautiful people. They could be exaggerating their problem areas (as if they were under a magnifying glass). They could be assuming that *other* people consider those features ugly — a form of mind-reading which is rarely valid. They could be feeling ugly because they're in a bad mood about other things and they're letting the bad feeling spill over into their judgment about their appearance.

So Rena may really have some unattractive features (as everyone does), but she's feeling ugly because she's concentrating her attention on those features while ignoring her attractive points (which everyone also has). For example, Rena's hair is a beautiful shade of gold; she's petite and delicate in her body type; her posture is excellent; her teeth are even and sparkly white; her eyelashes are thick and long; her fingers are long and graceful; and her face has a perfect, oval shape.

If Rena focused her attention on these positive attributes, she'd feel a lot happier about her appearance. Then, she might be willing to work with her "negative" assets in order to play them down — for example, using a bit of skin-colored medication to heal and cover up her blemishes, learning to style her hair so that its frizziness is obscured, finding the right chapstick to smooth and heal her lips, choosing more flattering glasses or switching to contact lenses. With a little effort and a lot of positive attitudes, Rena could feel and look like the beauty she really is.

SELF-ESTEEM

So you see, the Bad Judge causes a person to make errors in perception and judgment. Of course, everyone has a Bad Judge, but some people have a very large Bad Judge and others have quite a small one. A large Bad Judge constantly harps on all the things that are wrong about you: you're ugly, stupid, not good at things, not good at getting along with people, and so forth. If a person has a large Bad Judge giving him a lot of bad feelings, he is said to have low self-esteem.

Meet three young people — Dov, Elisheva, and Leah. See which one seems most like you.

Dov:

I guess you could say I'm an outgoing person. I like to be around people and it seems that people like to be around me, too — I mean, I have quite a few friends. I do pretty well in school. I'm not bad in sports. I'd say I was average looking, but I try to dress well so I look a little better. I'm pretty independent: I look after my own responsibilities (like my room at home, my homework, my activities). I'm more of a leader than a follower. I'm willing to stand apart from the crowd if the crowd is doing the wrong thing. For example, some of my pals laugh at me because I tend to defend and protect certain people who they make fun of. Look, I feel that no one deserves that kind of treatment, and I'm prepared to stand alone if necessary to make my point. Anyway, everyone has faults, including me, and that's no reason to pick on a person, is it?

Elisheva:

Well, I guess you'd say I'm not smart and not dumb. I'm not particularly good at anything — I mean I don't have any outstanding talents or anything like that. I'm ordinary. I don't have any really good friends; I sort of keep to myself. It's safer that way anyway because you avoid the chance of people putting you down or laughing at you. (I actually think I worry too much about what other people think about me, but, then again, I tend to worry about a lot of things.) I'm not very good looking. I guess I'm too fat. I diet occasionally but I don't really get anywhere at it. I must admit that I get depressed quite often — you know, I feel down in the dumps. Whatever I do never seems to work out. If I study for hours on end, I still don't get the grades I want. If I go out of my way to do something nice for people, they don't even notice it. I don't get along well with my mother. She criticizes me for every little thing—it drives me bananas. I really can't cope with it.

Leah:

Let's see, where shall I begin? I guess I should say that I'm a basically kind person (at least I never go out of my way to hurt anyone). I must admit, though, that I have a tendency to be moody—especially at home. I have one really good friend and a couple of so-so friends. I'm not Miss Popularity, but I don't really care. I'm a good student if I work at it, which I sometimes do and sometimes don't, depending on whether or not I like the subject. I don't think I'm very attractive: my legs are too fat, my face is funny-looking, and my skin is too dark. But what can a person do about the way he looks? I'm also not as physically active as I'd like to be; a lot of people I know are fantastic swimmers or agile dancers. I'm sort of a klutz. However, I can write short stories reasonably well and I do a lot of that in my spare time. I also enjoy reading, but I let my Mom pick out most of my library books for me. She's much better at it than I am. She also buys my clothes for me—I really don't know how to shop as well as she does. But we even it out because I do all the baking in our house—my Mom claims she can't make anything as well as I do!

Do You Have High Self-Esteem, Low Self-Esteem, or In-Between Self-Esteem?

Perhaps you are a lot like one of these people, or maybe you have a little of each of them in you. Dov sounds like a young man with pretty high self-esteem. He likes himself and he accepts himself, including his weak areas. He's not particularly worried about the opinion that others have of him. Elisheva has low self-esteem. Her Bad Judge has a lot of power, making plenty of negative assessments and predictions. She is insecure in a lot of ways, particularly about what other people think about her. Leah, on the other hand, is somewhere in-between. She has some unduly negative ideas about herself and her abilities (the Bad Judge in action!), but she also knows her areas of strength and competency.

What's the Difference Between High Self-Esteem and Haughtiness?

Some people get mixed-up when it comes to understanding self-esteem. They think that in order to be humble (which is a positive Jewish trait) they should have low self-esteem. They think that they should always put themselves down, saying, "I don't do this well," and "I don't do that well."

However, this is not true humbleness. In fact, this is more like lying! If you can do something well, it is only being honest with yourself if you admit it. And it is also being grateful to God to acknowledge any gifts, talents, beauty, or other benefits that He has given you. In addition, recognizing and accepting your strengths is the first step in accepting the responsibility that comes with them: the responsibility to use all of your abilities to better yourself and the world in which you live.

A person who has low self-esteem denies the things he can do and be. A person who has high self-esteem is aware of the things he can do well and is not afraid to face the things he can't do well. On the other hand, a person who is haughty is one who thinks that since he can do something well, he is better than other people. This is ridiculous of course. We all do certain things well and have certain things going for us. Just because you can accomplish something — let's say you are a terrific artist — does not mean that you are GREAT. It only means that you are a regular human being with a particular skill. You can feel good about having that skill (and all of the other capabilities that you have) while still being a humble person.

Thus, low self-esteem is not humbleness and high self-esteem is not haughtiness. Rather, low self-esteem is self-deception and high self-esteem is honesty and gratitude.

People do not purposely develop low self-esteem, however. Those who live around very critical people often develop a strong Bad Judge and correspondingly low self-esteem. It's also possible to have low self-esteem without being the victim of critical people, just by having mistaken ideas.

The good news is that it's possible to have high self-esteem no matter who you live with, no matter what kind of criticisms you have been subject to, and no matter what mistaken ideas you are holding, provided you learn how to shrink your Bad Judge and build up your Positive Power.

POSITIVE POWER

Your Positive Power is the part of you that thinks positive thoughts about your character and about what you can do. It is the part that takes care of you, preserving your strength for good things. With Positive Power, we face life optimistically and feel that we can meet its challenges.

Positive Power enables us to attain our purpose in life by fulfilling our potential in the world. Positive Power is energizing.

The voice of Positive Power says things like, "I can do it." "I'm good at it." "I'm okay." "I'm loveable." "I'm allowed to make mistakes." "I like myself." Positive Power gives us courage. For example, when standing in front of an audience to give a speech, the Bad Judge says, "i'll be a flop. i'll embarrass myself in front of everyone. i'll make a fool of myself. They'll hate my speech. i feel like running away!" Positive Power says, "I can do it. I think they'll really enjoy it. I'll just be myself. I'll be a success. And if I make some mistakes, that's okay too. Everyone has had that experience. I'll survive my mistakes and even learn from them."

Where do we get Positive Power from? It comes from inside your own head in two ways:

1) as a memory of things you were told by people who are important to you, and

2) as a conclusion that you drew from your own experiences.

Again, Positive Power acts like a series of tapes with messages assessing our performance and potential. For example, if someone has parents who frequently say things like, "That was a really clever answer to the question," he might create a Positive Power tape that says, "I can use my mind well." Or, someone who consistently gets good marks on his tests at school may create his own Positive Power tape that says, "I know that I can succeed."

Just like Bad Judge tapes, Positive Power tapes directly affect our behavior. Even though you may not hear the tape playing, your mind does hear it and directs your behavior to be consistent with its message. For example, if you have a Positive Power tape that says, "People like me," then when you find yourself in a situation where you have to meet new people, you will act confident, relaxed, and happy. If, however, you happened to have a Bad Judge tape which plays, "People don't like me," then you will act insecure, tense, and uncomfortable in the same situation — all this without even being consciously aware of the presence of your tapes!

CHANGING TAPES

We all have Bad Judge tapes and Positive Power tapes in our heads. As with any tape recorder, if you don't like the tapes, you can pull them out and put other ones in. You can play the "music" you want to hear. Sometimes a tape gets jammed in the machine and just won't come out. In that case, you can always adjust the volume — turn it up or turn it down. For example, if you hear a voice in your head saying, "i'm afraid to give my speech," you can turn the volume down on that voice (make it barely a whisper) while simultaneously turning the volume up on an appropriate Positive Power tape: "I'M GOING TO DO A GOOD JOB—I KNOW I CAN DO IT." The Positive Power tape should then drown out the Bad Judge tape!

Of course, the ideal thing is to completely pull out the Bad Judge tape whenever possible. For instance, suppose you're getting dressed for a wedding. As you stand in front of the mirror, you hear your Bad Judge saying, "i look terrible." As you hear this thought, you naturally begin to feel bad. That's because the thoughts we think cause us to feel feelings. Bad Judge thoughts cause us to feel sad, depressed, scared, unhappy, angry, and so forth. On the other hand, Positive Power thoughts cause us to feel happy, confident, calm, and so on.

Now, having heard your Bad Judge, you decide to pull out the tape and put a Positive Power tape in its place. YANK. Okay. Now you hear, "If I stand straight, I look a lot better." You feel a little better at hearing this, but not too much. So you turn up the volume much louder: "IF I STAND STRAIGHT, I LOOK A LOT BETTER!!" Ah-h-h. That's better. You throw in a few more Positive Power tapes: "My skin looks pretty clear today." "My hair is freshly washed — looks not bad." "My teeth are definitely white — they'll look great in a smile." The more tapes you throw in, the happier you start to feel.

Is it that easy?

Yes. You have total control of these tapes. You are not a victim of your past. You don't have to play the same old tapes that you've always played—you can put new ones on at any time. Of course, the new tapes always sound "strange" at first. After all, you're not used to hearing them. The old ones sound more familiar and more comfortable, even if they are Bad Judge tapes. So you keep them around and continue to play them even after you start playing replacement tapes. The more you play the new tapes, however, the more you get used to hearing them and the more natural they will come to feel. (You can play new tapes over and over again, just to get used to the sound. When you're working on a new tape, try playing it as many times a day as you possibly can.)

Also, the louder you play your tapes, the better you will hear and feel them. So SHOUT your new tapes in your head rather than mumble them weakly. After a while, the new tapes become the "new you." They become the tapes you want to play all the time. Eventually, you just throw the old ones in the garbage, never to be played again.

Sarah:

Here's how it happened with me. I had this thing about math. I never was good with numbers. My Bad Judge tape said, "i give up. i'll never add two and two and get four. i'll just buy a calculator and hope for the best." Of course, when I bought a calculator, my Bad Judge tape said, "What made me think i'd be able to use that thing? i know that i'm terrible with numbers. There's no point in trying."

I still had to take math classes in school, and naturally, I was failing miserably. One day, however, my teacher, Mrs. Gold, called me aside and said to me: "Sarah, you did quite well on this page of fractions." (She meant that I actually got some answers correct.) She added, "I think you're getting the hang of it." Well, I heard a very tiny Positive Power tape squeaking, "I'm beginning to get the hang of it." I sort of liked the sound of it, so I turned up the volume louder. The more I played it, the more I liked it. I decided that I'd try an experiment.

Every time I opened my math book, whether in class or at home, I put on that tape good and loud: "I'M BEGINNING TO GET THE HANG OF IT!" I noticed that I felt an immediate surge in confidence and a positive shift in attitude. Instead of immediately turning myself off because I had to look at numbers, I actually kept my mind open, just to see if I was really getting the hang of it! Okay, no miracles happened. I mean, I still had plenty of trouble understanding my work.

So I decided to throw on a few more Positive Power tapes like, "I can do it if I try," "I'll take my time," "It's okay to ask for help."

Well, after a while, I really began to notice a change. First of all, I was beginning to be able to tolerate math. Second, I was beginning to understand a few things. Third, I began to feel that there was more that I could do than I had previously thought. Now, I still pump myself with Positive Power tapes whenever I have to deal with numbers, and I can honestly tell you that I'm finally licking this math-phobia.

Josh:

Let me tell you about my experience with changing tapes. I was never good at socializing. Any time that I had to be in a situation that called for me to interact with two or more people at a time, I'd get really tense and uncomfortable. Now, when I learned about the Bad Judge, I realized that any time I had uncomfortable feelings, my Bad Judge must be lurking behind the scenes.

So, I had a little interview with myself late one night. I asked myself, "What's Mr. Bad Judge saying to me that's making me feel uncomfortable around people?" At first, I got just one answer: "i'm not good at making small-talk." Then I pushed and pushed for all the Bad Judge thoughts that were hiding out. I really turned up the volume on my inner tape recorder so that I could hear those messages that were lurking beneath the surface. Here's what I got: "i'm not an interesting person. People aren't attracted to me. i don't have much to offer. People don't understand me. People don't like me. i don't know what to say. i'm not good at socializing. i'm not fun. i'll say something stupid. i'm not on the same wavelength as other people."

Now let me explain something. I didn't know that I had all these thoughts until I asked myself! I just knew that I felt bad in social situations. Now that I understood that my Bad Judge tapes were causing me to feel uncomfortable, I made a conscious decision to pull them out and replace them with Positive Power tapes.

I actually wrote down on a piece of paper a list of messages that were Positive Power ones. I made up this list based on what I thought a very positive person would say about himself. Here's what I wrote: "I'm as interesting as anyone else. I can make myself attractive to people by smiling, looking and sounding interested in what they're saying, and joining in the conversation. I'm as likeable as anyone else. I have something to offer people. I can talk to people just like I talk to my family. I can relax and be fun just like I do at home. I can speak intelligently. If I make a mistake, it doesn't mean I'm stupid (everyone is entitled to make mistakes). I have a lot in common with the other members of the human race."

After writing these messages down, I decided to rehearse them throughout the day. Of course, they didn't ring true because they weren't the kind of thoughts I was used to, but I just said them to myself anyway. If I was walking along the street, I'd pick one message and say it over and over inside my head. If I was doing any chore which didn't require my full attention (like making my bed or preparing my breakfast) I'd pick one message and repeat it over and over silently. Before drifting off to sleep at night, I'd go over a few more.

After only a few days of this kind of rehearsing, I already noticed a change in the way I was feeling. I had a chance to actually test out the change a couple of weeks later when I had a bar mitzvah dinner to attend. For once, I was looking forward to going to such a gathering. And when I was there — what a difference! All that "brainwashing" seemed to really penetrate my mind, and they definitely affected my feelings. And because I felt better and more optimistic, I behaved in a different way too. Let's put it this way: I made eye contact with everyone I talked to! And I did talk to people and I did have a good time. So to top it all off, I made a new Positive Power tape: "I'm good at interacting in groups!"

Obviously, people can really change the way they feel and act by changing their tapes. Anyone can do it. The important thing is not to sabotage the procedure by allowing the Bad Judge to say something like, "You can't change what i tell you to feel. You have to keep these bad feelings your whole life long." Or, "It's too much work for you to change feelings. It'll be easier just to keep things the way they are." Or, "Only deep psychotherapy could change a person's feelings. This method can't possibly work." Remember, the Bad Judge doesn't want you to succeed.

The first thing to do, therefore, is play a Positive Power tape that gives you permission to change your tapes. Choose any one or more of the following for this purpose:

- *"I can let the bad feelings go. I'm entitled to feel great."*
- *"It takes work to change feelings, but the work is easy and the payoffs are great."*
- *"Small changes in thinking have the power to make large changes in personality."*

- *"I only say positive things to myself."*
- *"The pleasure I can get from succeeding in life vastly outweighs the comforts I can receive for failing."*

Or make up some of your own tapes that challenge whatever your Bad Judge has to say on the subject!

POSITIVE POWER TAPES

Let's look at some examples of Positive Power tapes that are useful for every person to have on hand. You may already have some of these in your tape bank and may be using them regularly. Perhaps some of the ones you have are on low volume and you only need to make them louder and stronger. There may also be some that you don't have yet and you want to add to your supply. You can add any of the ones you see here and any others that you think of by yourself. You are never too old to add new tapes.

1. "I'm Intelligent."

This Positive Power tape applies to everyone. There is no one who is not intelligent, and this includes people who have low scores on "intelligence" tests. Let's remember that intelligence tests only measure certain limited aspects of intelligence. Everybody — even tiny newborn babies — has intelligence of various kinds. Just because a person doesn't do particularly well with schoolwork doesn't mean he isn't intelligent! After all, textbook learning only taps a certain limited competency that people have. It does not reflect a person's total "smartness." Plenty of people who fail academically go on to make fantastically successful lives for themselves using the many kinds of intelligences that they possess. Similarly, there are people who do quite well in school but who lack intelligence in other aspects of life. We are all familiar with the "absentminded professor" type who is brilliant in class but can never find his pencils or books, or carry on a conversation about anything other than his small area of expertise.

So everybody is smart in different ways. Some people are smart with their ears: they remember almost everything they hear. In school they sail through just by listening to what is being said (they rarely have to study their notes). After a class or lecture, they can give the whole thing over word for word. When they're introduced to new people, they remember their names for years after. They can sing in perfect pitch.

Then there are those who are smart with their eyes. If they read it, they remember it. If they look at a map, they can figure out exactly where they are and how to get where they want to go. If they meet a person, they'll remember that person's face years later. After looking at a word, they know how to spell it. Given the opportunity, they can decorate a room or coordinate a wardrobe with style.

Some people are smart with their hands. They can catch or throw a ball with perfect aim. They can play a musical instrument. They can draw beautiful and realistic pictures. They can play piano. They can type like a whiz. They can style hair. They can sew up a storm. They can rewire a house, repair a carburetor, or build a desk.

There are people who are smart socially. They know how to get along with others. They know what makes other people tick. They are sensitive to the needs of other people. They know how to motivate people, influence people, care for people, encourage people, please people. They know how to communicate.

Some people are smart with their words. They know how to express themselves clearly. They learn languages easily. They are great public speakers. They write effective letters. They are natural poets or authors.

Then there are other kinds of "smartnesses" that don't fit into any neat categories: smartness for cooking and baking, for organizing, for computer programming, for creative activities, for exercising or dancing, for fishing, for hopscotch — and for a million other things.

With so many different kinds of intelligences, every person can surely find his own subset of smartness. No one has high intelligence in every area, and no one is without intelligence in every area! And most of us have some intelligence in each area rather than having areas with zero intelligence. For example, a person who can learn simple dances is more intelligent in that area than a person who can't learn even one dance. However, there are very few people who can't learn even one very simple dance. Moreover, once a person has succeeded in learning one dance, he can most likely go on to learn more dances if provided with the kind of time and teaching he needs. Just because a person needs more time than someone else does in order to learn something does not mean that he lacks intelligence! It only means that he needs more time (or specialized teaching techniques).

Since we are all intelligent, it should be fairly easy to develop a set of Positive Power tapes for this characteristic.

- *"I've learned millions of things in my life, from walking and talking to algebraic equations. I can learn well."*

- "When I ask questions, I can learn more."
- "It's normal to have high intelligence in some areas and lower intelligence in other areas."
- "I can solve problems."
- "I learned English, so I can learn another language."
- "I learned to count, so I can learn to do other things with numbers."
- "I learned to make scrambled eggs (grilled cheese / bread and butter / or whatever else I can make) so I can learn to prepare other meals."
- "I'm capable with my (hands, feet, nose, eyes, etc.)."
- "I can use my kind of smartness to make my life successful."

2. "I'm an Important and Valuable Person."

Judaism teaches that no soul is brought down to this world accidently or without purpose.[1] Each person has a unique role in the universal scheme of events and in his own small circle in life.

For example, each child is important to his parents. This is true whether or not the child and parents are getting along with each other. Every parent knows the truth of this statement.

You are important to your brothers and sisters — and this is also true regardless of whether you are feeling friendly toward them or they are feeling friendly toward you. They learn from you whether they are older or younger than you are. Their own self-image includes you. In other words, they see themselves as being part of a family of four or six or nine or whatever, and that number includes you! When a family portrait is taken, if one member were missing, the entire picture would lose some value. The family is only a family with each member in the picture, and each makes an important contribution to the experience and quality of the family. You therefore have a unique impact on all of the people whom you call "your family."

You are also important to your friends. They count on you. They enjoy being with you and they need you to fill their world. You are also important to your acquaintances and even to the strangers you encounter. You never know how your words or behavior have affected others, even when you've only interacted with them on a few occasions. I'm sure you, yourself, can think of people who have influenced you in some way even though you were not good friends with them.

You are important to the Jewish people. Each Jew counts. Each is so important that he is considered to be an entire world in his own right.[2] Each Jew has the potential to add light to the world through living a Jewish life. Moreover, each adds his unique contribution to his community. You leave your mark, whether it is in the area of giving to others, helping others, leading others, working with others, inspiring others, encouraging others, showing others the way, lightening their load, cheering them up — or whatever it may be. You are an essential part of the whole.

David:

Some days I feel really depressed. Nothing seems to be going right. My parents are picking on me; my brothers aren't talking to me; my teachers are cold as icebergs; my friends are nonexistent.

On those days I feel, "What's the use? Nobody cares if I'm here or not. I might as well be invisible."

The more I think these kinds of things, the worse I feel. I feel more and more insignificant, more and more alone. Then I feel more and more depressed.

David needs to play some Positive Power tapes about being important. Here's some he could choose from:

- *"There's only one me in the whole world."*
- *"I have a chance to improve the world on a large scale or on a small scale and that makes me very important."*
- *"Even if people don't show me or tell me that I'm important, I know that I am important because God made me: He obviously wants me to exist."*
- *"When people are mad at me or disappointed in me, it shows that I'm important to them. If I wasn't, they wouldn't waste time or energy having ANY feelings toward me — positive or negative!"*
- *"Since I can't read other people's minds, I have no right to assume that they don't consider me important."*
- *"I can safely assume that I am important to many people — family members, friends, and people in my community."*
- *"I can make myself important to people by caring about them and being involved with them. The more I give to others, the more important I will become to them."*

3. "My Body Is Fine the Way It Is."

As we have already seen, the Bad Judge can play a big role in a person's body image (the way he views his body). When the Bad Judge speaks, a person can feel that he's too tall, too fat, too freckled, too plain, and altogether too unattractive! Here's Bryna's experience.

Bryna:

I've always been interested in clothes — how they look and how to put them together well and things like that. I study the models in the store windows, the ladies on magazine covers in the store, and the real-life "smart-dressers" at school, in the streets, and at shul. The only problem is that I myself don't have the figure for clothes. I mean, everyone I'm looking at is medium height, skinny, and beautiful, whereas I'm tall and wide around the waist. You could say I have a square shape. Even my face is sort of square instead of that nice oval shape the models all have.

Anyway, I used to get quite upset about this and I'd diet to the point of near-starvation so that my waist would get smaller (which it never did), and I'd slouch to make myself shorter, and I'd drape my hair down the sides of my face to make it look skinnier (but I only ended up looking sloppy!). And the whole time I just felt mad: why couldn't I have the perfect body? Why was I stuck with this losing form?

One day I was complaining about this to a good friend of mine, and she said something quite interesting. She told me that I was being ridiculous for wanting someone else's body and my body was fine the way it was. She pointed out that everybody has a different body shape: some people have long legs and others have short; some people have thick legs and others have thin; some people have skinny waists but lots have wide ones like mine, and so on. We don't all have to look like each other. And no one way of looking is better than any other. We can look like ourselves and still look beautiful.

From then on, I decided to think one positive thought every time I stood in front of a mirror: "I have my own personal beauty." With that thought as encouragement, I've been able to bring out the best in myself. I pick clothes that are flattering to MY body shape instead of trying to force my body into clothes that look good on another kind of person. I get my hair cut in a style which works WITH my facial features instead of one which tries to change my face. Whereas I used to feel unhappy about my hair all the time because it's thinner and straighter than the hair I see in the store windows, I've come to accept it as MINE and okay the way it is. All in all, I enjoy my body a lot more now that I accept it.

Bryna's one Positive Power tape — "I have my own personal beauty" — is truly a powerful message which can build confidence and attractiveness in anyone who uses it. Here are some others you may want to draw on as well:

- *"Just as my fingerprints are unique, so my entire body is unique."*
- *"Interior beauty (the beauty of my personality) makes my exterior beautiful."*
- *"There are as many ways of being beautiful as there are people in the world."*
- *"There will always be some people who like the color of*

my eyes or my hair or the shape of my body, and there will be others who don't. Since I must live with myself, I choose to be one of the people who approve of the way I look."

- *"I can always make myself completely beautiful just by wearing a big smile."*
- *"When I stand up straight and tall, my body looks its very best."*
- *"I don't have to have a 'perfect' body in order to be beautiful; my body is perfectly beautiful even with its imperfections."*

4. "I Am Entitled to Make Mistakes and Benefit from Them."

The Bad Judge doesn't permit you to make mistakes. It says, "Boy, am i dumb!" or "i'll never figure out how to do this," or "i'm the only one in the world who can't do this," or "i can never show my face again after making such a fool of myself!"

On the other hand, Positive Power gives permission to be human, to make errors and do things wrong. It encourages a person to stand up after making a mistake, dust himself off, and think about what went wrong. All mistakes have educational value. Of course, not all people use the opportunity lurking within an error. For example, read about Elisa's experience and see the two possible responses, described by Elisa-A and Elisa-B.

Elisa:

I was taking sewing lessons for the first time. We were making a simple skirt, but my Mom wanted it to be really

Understanding Yourself

nice so she bought some very attractive, expensive material for the project. The sewing teacher showed us (a class of six girls) how to lay out our patterns for cutting, and then left us on our own to get started. I thought I understood what was supposed to be done, so I eagerly pinned everything in place and started cutting away. All of a sudden, I realized that I had cut along a line that said, "Place on fold of material" — which means, "Don't cut along this line!"

I was sure I had ruined the entire skirt because there certainly wasn't enough material left on which to cut out the piece properly. However, my teacher said we could save the project by sewing the two pieces together, and even though the seam shouldn't really be there, the skirt would still be wearable.*

Now Elisa-A continues from *:

i felt really bad about it. How could i have been so stupid? i knew I shouldn't have taken sewing lessons — i obviously lacked talent. Even though i had to finish this set of classes, i decided then and there never to take any more lessons and never to sew again.

Now Elisa-B continues from *:

I realized that I made that mistake because I had been rushing. I didn't take the time to read the pattern carefully. I guess I was just a bit too enthusiastic. Well, I decided to slow down and be more careful when I cut patterns in the future. And from that time on, I have never made that kind of mistake again. Of course, I have made lots of other mistakes in sewing — but that's why they invented that handy little tool called a "seam-ripper" (it's for removing stitches that you put in by mistake, and they must have invented it because lots of people besides me make mistakes). Anyway, I keep on sewing and I'm getting better and better at it all the time. And I really enjoy it, too!

Elisa-A felt bad about her mistake. She didn't use it as a chance to learn something — she didn't want to look at it and see where she went wrong. She just felt bad about it and refused to try again. Her Bad Judge says, "i give up. i have no talent for sewing." In this way, Bad Judge tapes destroy a person's potential and stop them from accomplishing what they might be capable of.

On the other hand, Positive Power tapes help a person to develop all of his skills and abilities. Elisa-A never does learn to sew, while Elisa-B acquires a life-long skill which is both useful and pleasurable. Elisa-A feels that mistakes are a sign of failure, while Elisa-B sees them as an opportunity for growth.

Here are some Positive Power tapes on making mistakes:

- *"I'm allowed to make mistakes because I'm a human being and that's what human beings do."*
- *"Any mistake that I make has been made by thousands of people before me and will be made by thousands more after me."*
- *"When I make a mistake in public, I can remind myself that other people have also made this same kind of mistake publicly."*
- *"Everybody makes mistakes in every area of life, even in mitzvah observance. We are allowed to make mistakes, acknowledge them, be sorry for them, and ask forgiveness for them."*

- *"After I have made a mistake and analyzed it, I don't have to keep reminding myself about it. There's no need to suffer over past mistakes; I can forgive myself and move on."*
- *"If I don't try, I won't make any mistakes. But then, I won't succeed either."*
- *"Each mistake I make helps me learn something I didn't know before."*
- *"I like to think of myself as a problem-solver. Doing things wrong is just part of the process of figuring out how to solve a problem. Eventually I'll get it right and then go on to solve my next problem."*

5. "I'm a Successful Person."

All people are successful in as many ways as they allow themselves to be. Being successful is a matter of reaching one's potential in a given area. Since each human being is born with numerous "potentials" there are many areas in which each person can achieve success.

However, Bad Judge tapes interfere with the achievement of success. One way is by refusing to acknowledge accomplishments. If someone tells Tova that she sang really nicely in the school choir, her Bad Judge answers: "No, i made a mess of it. i could have done a lot better." If someone tells Dov that he's really bright, his Bad Judge says, "You're just saying that to flatter me. It's not really true." Both of these folks need to pull out their Bad Judge tapes and insert a Positive Power tape that accepts compliments, praise, and success and says, "Thanks."

Ignoring previous successes is one of the most damaging tactics of the Bad Judge when it comes to trying new things. Essentially, the Bad Judge pretends that you've never done anything right before, so you won't be able to succeed at your new task either. You open up a new page of mathematics, for instance, and your Bad Judge screams, "i can't do it!" before you even glance at the page. It has you convinced that you "can't do things." Positive Power tapes will remind you that you have a long history of successes — that you have succeeded at doing hundreds of "new pages" of math, for instance — and encourage you to try this one too. Positive Power will give you an "I can do it" message.

The Bad Judge prevents success in yet another way. It notices everything that you do wrong and refuses to notice the things you do right. For example, Ruth explains the difficulty she is having in making friends at her new school with these Bad Judge tapes.

Ruth:

i know why nobody likes me here. It takes me forever to make friends because i'm too quiet. i don't have any special talents that would make anyone notice me; i don't have really nice clothes or anything like that, and i'm plain looking in general. i guess you could say i'm boring.

Now Ruth may be describing her weaknesses pretty accurately, but she's only looking at the negative side of things. As it turns out, Ruth is a great person to be friends with because she is sensitive, understanding, funny, trustworthy, smart, caring, and generous. When someone gets to know her, they find all this out and really appreciate her.

However, Ruth's low opinion of herself, as voiced by her

Bad Judge, makes her feel insecure in approaching people. Therefore, she acts in a way that keeps people distant. For instance, she doesn't talk much, she keeps her eyes down to the ground, and she slouches. Eventually, she'll get to know someone by being assigned a project to work on with them or by sitting beside them for a year, but it's a slow way to make friends.

Ruth needs to play Positive Power tapes for herself so that she will feel more confident. For example: "I've got a lot to offer people. I listen well. I help people. I share my time, energy, and belongings. I tell good jokes and stories. I can keep a secret. I know a lot of interesting things to do." As she feels better, she'll stand up straighter, look people in the eyes, smile, and even talk to people. This way, she'll soon have plenty of friends. Positive Power tapes give a true picture of a person's strengths. When we can accept our good points graciously, we feel more successful and we're able to act in ways that increase our success even further.

Similarly, the Bad Judge can prevent our success by assuming the worst about ourselves. For example:

> Benny is walking down the street and notices his friend Saul on the other side of the road, walking with another young man. Benny waves to Saul, but Saul doesn't wave back. Benny's Bad Judge tapes take off: "i guess he's embarrassed to be seen saying hello to me. Or maybe he's just not interested in talking to me — i'm probably a nobody to him. He probably wishes i weren't walking down the street now."
>
> As these tapes play, Benny starts to feel angry and depressed. Fortunately, Benny knows about Positive Power tapes and realizes, just in time, that he'd better

pull out the Bad Judge and put in a Positive Power. Now he hears, "Stay calm. I know that Saul's a good friend of mine and that I'm an okay, likeable person. There's a couple of reasons that could explain why Saul didn't wave back. For one thing, he's very short-sighted and it's quite possible he didn't recognize me, or maybe didn't even see me. Or maybe he was so engrossed in his conversation with the other fellow that he didn't notice anything or anyone around him. I know that Saul would be happy to greet me if he saw me." As these Positive Power tapes play, Benny immediately relaxes and feels fine.

In fact, Benny really should be judging his friend Saul positively,[3] by assuming that there's some logical, positive reason why he didn't greet him. Moreover, Benny should be judging himself positively as well,[4] assuming that he is a likeable, agreeable person! There are so many times that we allow the Bad Judge to put us down, making us feel negatively about ourselves and our potential for successful relationships and undertakings. Positive Power pats us on the back, reminds us of our strengths, and encourages us for the future.

Here are some useful Positive Power tapes for being successful:

- *"I'm already successful in many ways."*
- *"It's good to admit my strengths and areas of accomplishment — it helps me succeed even more."*
- *"It is good to enjoy my successes, and doing so does not make me a 'proud' person; everyone has both successes and failures to deal with — therefore, acknowledging what I do well is fine as long as I also acknowledge what I need to improve in."*

- *"I have many successful personal qualities; I can assume that people will be attracted to me."*
- *"I can do what I set out to do. I'm a winner."*
- *"I can make other people feel good by accepting their compliments graciously (i.e., saying 'Thank you')—whereas rejecting people's praise can make them feel foolish. Accepting someone's compliment lets him know that I respect his judgment and taste."*

6. "I'm Okay the Way I Am."

How is this possible? Suppose a person does many things wrong—he lies, cheats, steals, and hurts people. Is he okay the way he is? Yes and no.

No, his behavior is not okay.[5] He must work to change his actions and learn to behave properly.[6] And yet, even this liar, cheater, and thief is okay in his essence. After all, he wasn't born behaving in this manner, and even if he had some inborn bad tendencies, he always retains his free choice to improve and perfect himself.[7] He was born as a totally acceptable baby, made just the way God wanted him to be. His nature was, and still is, okay. His hair color and eye color are fine the way they are. His height, his facial features, his foot size are all okay. His tendencies to be very active, boisterous, and funny (or whatever his temperamental characteristics happen to be) are all just fine. The fact that he can't carry a tune is all right too. So is the fact that he has trouble remembering details, and that he never did learn to read fluently, and that he has terrible handwriting. These things are not in his control and certainly don't make him any less okay.

The nature of a person, including his talents and abilities, and weaknesses and disabilities, are given to him by God.[8] Any such characteristics and positions, including a person's appearance, level of intelligence, and his wealth, are by definition okay.

The question a person must ask himself is, "Am I doing the best I can with what I have to work with?" Nobody's perfect, of course. The main thing is to aim in the right direction and keep trying.

Some people do not think they're okay the way they are, and they waste time trying to improve in areas that don't count for them. For example, here's what Esther thinks.

Esther:
Unfortunately, I'm very ordinary compared to my sisters. My older sister, Elana, is very talented and popular. She's always a leading character in our school plays. She has a million invitations on Shabbos afternoons; the telephone is always ringing for her. And she's gorgeous. I mean her hair is always stunning and stays neatly in place, her complexion is clear and rosy, and her figure is perfect.

Then there's my younger sister, Sari. She's brilliant. She never has to study but she always gets straight A's. Her character is impeccable: her middle name is "kindness." She helps my parents do everything; she babysits for neighbors for free; she organizes campaigns for unfortunate people; her idea of fun is to collect clothes and send them off to needy Jews in other lands.

Then there's me. i'm too short and too fat. i'm shy, so i don't have that many friends. i have to work my head off to get very average marks in school. i know i'm moody and a bit kvetchy — no one would call me a perfect angel. I mean, I do have some good points too, but they're not very exciting. Like, I'm a pretty good cook. And I'm a very good listener — a lot of people come to me with their problems. I know how to sew a little, which no one else in the family does.

I really try to be like my sisters. I stand in front of the mirror for hours, trying to get my hair right. I scrub my face a hundred times a day and spend almost all my allowance on skin creams so that my complexion will look half as good as Elana's. I wish I could make more friends but i just don't know how. I study as hard as I can, but as I mentioned, i don't do very well. I try and join in Sari's kindness campaigns, but it's obvious that she's always the leader and i'm just sort of tagging along. No matter what i do, i can't live up to their standards. i'm a flop."

Esther couldn't be further from the truth! She does not have to be like her sisters in order to be okay. She's perfectly okay as she is. If God gave her average looks and average intelligence and a quiet nature, instead of outstanding looks and superior intelligence and an outgoing nature, then these must be the qualities she needs in order to fulfill her own unique mission in this world. Trying to be like someone else is like trying to fulfill *their* purpose — a futile endeavor!

Each person has only one task: to use whatever nature he has been given in order to reach his own potential, to accomplish his own mission.

> A student came to his rebbe and complained to him about all that he was lacking in his character traits. He said, "If I had the mind of the Shaagas Aryeh (a

Talmudic genius) and the character traits of Rabbi Yisrael Salanter (who was renowned for his kindness), then I could serve God properly."

The rebbe answered him, "Had God wanted you to serve him with those traits, he would have given them to you. He wants you to serve Him with the traits that YOU have."

If we look around we will always find people who are more gifted, beautiful, wealthy, sociable, and talented than we are; and we will also find people who are less gifted, beautiful, wealthy, sociable, and talented than we are. We shouldn't try to be like any of these people because we are okay just as we are. Here are some Positive Power tapes to reinforce this idea:

- *"I don't have to be outstanding in order to be okay."*
- *"I don't have to compare myself to others — I'm fine the way I am."*
- *"I'm okay even though I'm not perfect. Nobody is perfect and nobody is supposed to be perfect."*
- *"I have a lot of very fine qualities."*
- *"I have advantages and disadvantages in my nature, just like everyone else has."*
- *"My only job is to make myself the best version of ME that I can — I don't have to be anyone else in order to be successful."*

7. "I Am Loveable."

Since there is a commandment to love our fellow Jews,[9] we must assume that all Jews are loveable. After all, we are not told to go and find some Jews whom we deem loveable (after considering all of their good points and their bad points) and then go and love *those* people. No. We are supposed to love one another without judging — without trying to decide who deserves our love.

This means that *you* are loveable. No matter what human faults and failings you may have, you are still a loveable person. If a person had to be perfect in order to be loved, then no one would ever be loved (since none of us is perfect). Not only do we not have to be perfect, we do not have to be special in any way. Just because we are here, we deserve to be loved.

Although this is true, some people act toward their children, brothers and sisters, parents, friends, or acquaintances in ways which say, "I don't love you." Of course, this is wrong. And acting in such a way can cause a person to feel unlovable. Take Shayna, for example.

Shayna:

My mother criticizes me a lot. Maybe she doesn't realize it; maybe she doesn't mean it. I don't know. But I do know that I feel like two cents around her. She may tell you that she loves me, but I know it's not true. Nobody who loves you picks on you so much. And if your own mother can't love you, then there must be something the matter with you. I mean, she'd love me if I was loveable, wouldn't she?

Shayna is feeling unlovable because of the way her mother acts toward her. However, she is loveable even if her mother (or anyone else) tells her in actions or words that she is not. Shayna is deciding that she doesn't deserve to be loved because one person — albeit a very important person — is acting in a way which says, "I don't love you."

In fact, even if many people were to give Shayna an I-don't-love-you message, this would not mean she wasn't loveable. It could mean one of two things:

1) the people are accidently communicating rejection even though they don't really feel this way, or

2) the people are purposefully communicating rejection because Shayna has been making herself unlikable through her behavior.

Shayna needs to realize that people may lack skill or ability to communicate their love and that this does not take away from her own lovableness. She also needs to know that even if her own behavior is unlikable at a given point in time, she is still deserving of the basic respect and kindness with which all people are to be treated because they are loveable in their essence.

When we fulfill the commandment to love our fellow Jews, we treat people the way we would like to be treated.[10] For example, we share the happiness of others, help them in times of trouble, forgive them for hurting us, teach them what they need to know, warn them about dangers, give them good advice, speak kindly to them, be considerate of them, judge them positively, be patient with them, give them pleasure, and do whatever else would bring happiness and comfort to them — since this is what we all want for ourselves. This is how we are supposed to act toward all people, including all the members of our family. And this is the way all people are supposed to act toward us. All people are loveable.

Shayna can throw out her Bad Judge tapes and replace them with the following Positive Power tapes:

- *"I deserve to be treated in a loving way because God says so."*
- *"Even if I do things wrong and need to be corrected, I deserve to be corrected in a loving way (with respect for my feelings)."*
- *"Even if someone doesn't treat me in a kind, loving fashion, I am still loveable."*
- *"If my parents don't speak to me in a loving way, it doesn't necessarily mean that they don't love me, and it definitely does not mean that I'm not loveable." (See more about this in the chapter "Understanding Parents.")*

8. "I Am Allowed to Have My Feelings."

People have emotions. They experience happiness, grief, anger, fear, confusion, hurt, and many other feelings. It would be terrible if we didn't have feelings like these; we would be like robots going through the actions of living without feeling truly alive.

Everyone likes "positive" feelings — moments of joy, laughter, pleasure, and satisfaction. No one enjoys the "negative" feelings — the times of worry, pain, humiliation, anger, frustration, and sadness. However, we all have all of these feelings, and each feeling serves a positive purpose.

How can negative emotions have a positive purpose? Let's say a child had only one emotion — happiness. Having no negative emotions such as fear, he might play in the middle of traffic or walk right into a burning fire! Never feeling disappointment, he would be content to fail all his tests in school, and he would never feel the need to improve his study habits. He'd never be sad, so he wouldn't mind at all if his best friend moved away. If someone in his family got sick, he wouldn't worry and he wouldn't do anything to help them get better!

So we can see that negative feelings can actually help a person to live properly. We need them at the right times. We don't need them at the wrong times. In other words, there is a right time to feel anger, a right time to feel sadness, and a right time to feel every other negative emotion.[11] If a good friend moves away, for example, this is a right time to be sad — your sadness will move you to write letters and maintain the bond of friendship. If your country has just declared war, this is a right time to be afraid — your fear will prompt you to pray to Hashem for help.

However, the Bad Judge can make us feel angry, sad, or scared at the wrong times. For example, fifteen-year-old Aliza is afraid to borrow sugar from a neighbor for her mom because her Bad Judge says, "i can't talk to adults because they'll think i'm strange." The bad feeling that Aliza gets from her Bad Judge is very real. Hopefully, somebody can help Aliza to use Positive Power tapes to feel more confident and courageous about such errands. But nobody should tell her that she's silly (or dumb or bad) to feel the way that she does. She's allowed to feel her feelings because they are really there. Aliza, herself, wants to stop having such feelings because all negative feelings are uncomfortable. With the right teacher, she can learn how to stop feeling badly when it's not necessary or appropriate.

Moshe:
I'll never forget this experience: I was eight years old. I had a really bad toothache, so my mother sent me to the

dentist. The dentist said my tooth was abscessed and had to be removed right away. I'd never had anything more than a check-up at the dentist before this, and I was very afraid of getting my tooth pulled. I started getting very upset, crying and screaming. The dentist told me to stop crying. He said I was a big boy and I shouldn't be scared. He made me feel like a real baby, but I just couldn't help myself: I was terrified. After he pulled my tooth, he told my mother that I was just faking and that nothing hurt me at all.

The dentist was trying to make Moshe's bad feelings go away by telling him that they were not necessary. However, he probably would have been more successful at calming Moshe down if he had just accepted the child's feelings as natural and understandable. For example, the dentist could have said something like, "I know it's scary having a tooth pulled for the first time. We have to do it because.... Here's exactly what's going to happen...." After all, Moshe was a little boy encountering a new and potentially painful experience. It was very normal for him to be afraid and upset.

Similarly, it is very normal for all people to feel moody at times, or depressed for a while, or nervous, or worried. These feelings can prompt us to take action to improve our situations. However, if such negative feelings last for a long time, it is best to seek help to replace Bad Judge tapes with Positive Power tapes. Whether the feelings last a long time or are short-lived, they should be acknowledged and accepted, and then they can be dealt with. In fact, the occurrence of "bad" feelings is so common that we are encouraged to prepare ourselves mentally for their arrival even when things are going well.[12] Expecting the flow of positive and negative days in the normal experience of living helps one to accept the gloomy moments more gracefully, with less shock, disappointment, and pessimism.

Here is Ruth's experience of "bad moods."

Ruth:

Sometimes I get irritable for no reason. If my little brother asks me to pass the salt, I might say in a rather nasty tone of voice something like, "Get it yourself, lazybones!" Then my older sister inevitably gets into the act. She'll say, "What's the matter with you? Didn't you get enough sleep last night?" That just makes me madder. But if my mother is around and overhears this conversation, she'll come to my rescue. She normally says something like, "Oh, Ruthie is having growing pains tonight. Honey, even if you're feeling irritable, please speak nicely to your brother, okay?" That makes me feel better, because I know my mom understands my moods — she calls them my growing pains because she says that teenagers tend to get moody as they grow into adults. Of course, she's right that I shouldn't take things out on everybody in the house, that I should learn to control myself. So, I continue feeling irritable inside but I try to behave myself. After a while I loosen up and feel a lot better. My moods always pass.

Ruth's mother is wise to acknowledge her feelings. It would be painful to Ruth if her mom would have said, "Cheer up, Ruth. We don't like sourpusses around here!" Since Ruth feels irritable, there's no use denying it or ordering her to feel differently. It helps a lot more if the feeling is just accepted and dealt with.

Understanding Yourself

To help you accept all of your feelings and handle them in healthy ways, try some of these Positive Power tapes:

- *"It's normal to get angry once in a while (normal but not desirable) — even so, I should never hurt people with my words or actions."*
- *"Even when I get very upset, I'm still in full control of my words and actions."*
- *"It's normal to feel down for a few days. I'll be back in a better mood soon."*
- *"It's natural to be afraid of new experiences. I'll do some research (read, ask people questions) about this upcoming experience to help prepare myself and make myself feel more relaxed."*
- *"I can feel as happy as I want to. Happiness is good for me physically, emotionally, and spiritually."*
- *"Feeling discouraged is normal. I can play some Positive Power tapes to help me overcome discouragement whenever I want to."*
- *"When I find myself worrying, I can pull out my Bad Judge tapes that are telling me about all the things that will go wrong and put in some Positive Power tapes that can tell me about all the things that will go right!"*

9. "I Can Take Care of Myself."

Another excellent Positive Power tape is the message that you can take care of yourself. Basically, this tape helps keep a person functioning well. It puts a quick end to negative moods; it keeps a person cheerful and successful.

You see, the best person to take care of you is — you!

You really know what you need in order to feel good and you are the one most able to make things happen the right way. Here's how Michael explains it.

Michael:

There was a big turning point in my life when I finally realized that I could make myself happy. Before that, I used to blame my unhappiness on everything and everyone around me. If I didn't work hard in school, I blamed the teacher (I'd say that the teacher didn't like me or I didn't like the teacher, and that's why there was no point studying that subject). If I was in a bad mood at home, I'd say it was because my mother was picking on me. If I was lonely, I'd say that all the kids were snobs.

Then I happened to read a book about optimism. This book explained how to take charge of your life and make things happen the way you want them to. A lot of it had to do with thinking the right way — looking for solutions to problems (instead of giving up), looking for the good side of things, talking about good news instead of bad news, and things like that. But the most important point for me was the idea of DOING something to cheer yourself up. The book said that a person should pull himself out of a bad state by doing those things which would make him feel good. It's not up to someone else to make you happy; it's up to yourself.

Once I started to put these ideas into practice in my own life, I felt the power of control. Now I am my own boss. I can't control what happens to me, but I sure can control how I will respond to it.

What Michael has discovered is that he doesn't have to be a passive victim of his circumstances. He has learned to ask himself the question, "What will make me feel good/better right now?" He answers this question and then does whatever he needs to do.

For example, let's say that his teacher looks at his rough draft of a major research assignment and says, "That's just not good enough Michael. It needs a lot more research and a lot more work." In the past, Michael would go home, tear up his assignment, and just not hand one in. He would claim it was the teacher's fault that he got a failing grade on this paper (because the teacher was too mean, too discouraging, too unfair, or whatever else). Now, however, Michael asks himself what he needs to do in order to feel better. He admits that he would enjoy getting a good mark on this paper. Even though he doesn't like this teacher too much, he decides to use the teacher to get the mark he wants. He asks the teacher what he needs to do, exactly, in order to fix his assignment and make it a grade-A paper. The teacher tells him; he does it; he gets top marks.

Michael knows how to take care of himself. A person can take care of himself in any situation. Even a person who is sick in bed, Heaven forbid, has the option of taking care of himself. He can ask someone to bring him some humorous books to read or funny tapes to listen to (laughter is the best medicine!).[13] He may be able to call a friend and have an interesting or uplifting conversation. He may be able to get out some markers and draw some silly, happy, beautiful, or encouraging pictures. He may be able to write his own funny poems or stories. In fact, when a person is feeling down for whatever reason, he can also do these kinds of things.

There are lots of things to do when you're feeling blue

or irritable or upset. Here's Elisa's list.

Elisa:

These are my favorite things to do to take care of myself and cheer myself up:
- *dress up extra nicely*
- *do some vigorous exercise or go for a quick walk*
- *put on some up-beat music*
- *talk to my Mom*
- *take a bubble bath*
- *make a delicious, but nutritious, snack*
- *call a friend and go out*
- *play with the little kids in the family*
- *cook or bake a special treat*
- *read something inspirational*

I'll pick one of these things to do, and if I'm not feeling better in a short while, then I'll try another. Even if I'm in the worst mood EVER, I'll always feel better once I've done three things on my list!

Everyone can make a list of things that work for him. The important thing is to use it whenever you notice that a negative feeling is lasting longer than you want it to. Here are some Positive Power tapes that can help you take action to take care of yourself:

- *"I'm the expert on what makes me feel good so I can do the best job of cheering myself up."*
- *"I can ask for what I want from people. Chances are good that I'll get what I ask for. If I don't, I'm no worse off for asking."*
- *"If I want to wait for someone to cheer me up or for my*

situation to change, I may have a long wait. I'd rather be happy now."

- *"Even when I'm down, I can use the little tiny part that always stays optimistic to pull myself up. It's like a little match that gets a big fire going. Once I take a tiny step in the right direction, things start rolling on their own and I'm soon feeling great again."*

10. "I Can Make a Decision."

This is the final Positive Power tape that we shall discuss. This tape is a real confidence booster. People who are willing to take risks and deal with the consequences soon come to feel competent to live life. They learn that they can handle whatever comes their way. What a great feeling!

Decision making involves risk taking. That's okay. There's no way to live without taking risks. Just walking out the front door in the morning involves plenty of risks. Even staying in bed all day involves certain risks (Will an earthquake make the house cave in? Will food arrive?). However, most people don't think about the risks that affect them until they are faced with a decision.

Should I buy the blue dress or the green one? No big risk here. But I might look better in the green. Or maybe I'll look better in the blue. I might be making a mistake and buy the one that doesn't look best on me. Then what?

Life is full of small decisions like that. Some people agonize over such decisions every day. They are afraid to commit themselves either way. They think that they can avoid failure by avoiding making a decision. The truth is just the opposite! Making the decision and living with it (no matter how it turns out) builds success. If the decision doesn't work out the way you hoped, then you learn from your experience. If it does, then you learn from that, too. There's no failure. Every decision helps you to increase your skills and competence in living.

Even those who don't worry about small decisions sometimes have problems with the bigger ones. Here's Deena's dilemma.

Deena:

I have a real problem. My best friend Miriam confided in me that she did a bad thing. She cheated on the mid-term math exam by looking at her neighbor's answers. She told me that even though she doesn't understand the material at all, she's going to get a really good grade in the class. Miriam made me promise not to tell anybody about this. Later, however, I realized that maybe I have some kind of obligation to tell someone. I don't know what to do.

Deena is in a difficult situation. She needs to make some kind of decision about what she's going to do. She can follow these basic procedures for making any decision — large or small — to help her resolve this conflict:

1) Get information from experts: parents, teachers, friends, or books.

2) Write down all the possible solutions you can think of.

3) Write down the advantages of each possible solution.

4) Write down the disadvantages of each possible solution.

5) Take your time in making the decision.

6) When applicable, consult a competent Torah authority for direction.

A decision like Deena's requires expert input because

it involves an issue of "right" and "wrong." Deena is not in a position to make that kind of decision on her own. She needs to consult the right people — her parents or a rabbi. They'll let her know how she should proceed.

However, many typical decisions are easily solved using steps 1 to 5. For example, Alexander has a decision to make.

Alexander:

I had the choice of going away to camp for a month or working here in the city. Both were appealing to me, and I didn't know what to do. The decision was completely up to me because my parents didn't mind either way.

I took a piece of paper and I wrote down all the pros and cons for each option. For example, I wrote down that camp was a good option because I'd get lots of fresh air and sunshine. I wrote down that it was not so good because I wouldn't make any money there. I wrote down that working in the city was a good option because I'd earn the money that I want to put toward owning my own car. I put down that it was not so good because I'd miss my friends a lot. I kept writing down the advantages and disadvantages until I couldn't think of any more. Then I added up each side. It turned out that the "camp" option had three advantages and three disadvantages. The "work in the city" option had four advantages and six disadvantages. Even though the "work in the city" option had one more advantage, I felt that the extra disadvantages really mattered. I decided to go to camp.

Sometimes just the process of writing down the options and their pros and cons can lead a person to make his decision. Other times, adding up the points on each side is necessary. When the points are added, remember to double or triple those that are *really* important to you. For example, if Alexander felt that the money was really crucial, he might have tripled its point value. That way, even if it turned out that money was the only advantage he listed on his sheet, it would be equal to three advantages of the camp option.

Some people find it more useful to just talk about the options to someone else, instead of writing them down on paper. Then, having heard themselves think out loud about the problem, they are in a position to make a decision.

Once the decision is made and acted upon, it can be evaluated. This means that you can now assess whether or not you are satisfied with the choice you made. For example, Alexander can look back over the summer and ask himself if his expectations of camp were met. Is he happy, after all, that he decided to go? If camp was not as successful as he anticipated, he might then say to himself, "Well, I'm disappointed. Maybe I would have been more satisfied in the city after all. Next year I'll remember that camp isn't quite as gratifying as I thought it would be." This will help Alexander make a decision next year.

Most decisions, fortunately, are not in the "life-or-death" category. Nothing terrible will happen even if things don't turn out as hoped for. Here are Mimi's thoughts on the subject.

Mimi:
Since I've been more willing to make decisions, I've noticed a "bonus." I find that I don't worry as much! Everybody always made fun of me because I'm such a big worrier. They say "worry" is my middle name! However,

since I've learned to make decisions and calmly analyze the results of those decisions, I've found that I can apply the same process to anything that I would normally worry about. For example, if I had exams coming up, I'd spend a lot of time worrying about them. But now I can think out my options, just like I was making a decision. I say, "I can study or I can worry. If I study, I'll have to work hard but I'd probably get good marks. If I don't study, I'll have it easy now, but I'll regret it when I get my report card. Since regretting it is really worth 3 disadvantage points, I think I'd better study now and do as well as I can." Then I just do it.

If the thing I'm worrying about is not in my control, I still use my decision-making skills to handle it. For example, let's say I'm worried because my younger sister has borrowed my good sweater and she might ruin it. So I think to myself, "If she ruins it she'll pay me for a new one. The new one might be even nicer than this one. If she doesn't ruin it, I'll get to enjoy it for longer." I guess just being in the habit of thinking and of looking for advantages helps to cure irrational emotions like worrying. Anyway, it works for me.

Here are some Positive Power tapes to help you make decisions:

- "I can live with the results of any decision I make."
- "I don't have to be 'right' on every decision I make. That would be inhuman. Human beings make some good decisions and some bad ones. I can learn from all of them."
- "When I make a decision, I can get on with life."

- *"When I make a decision, I close many doors (since I reject the other options). However, I open one. It's always fun to see what's inside the room of the opened door."*
- *"My decisions don't have to be perfect. I can be satisfied with the good aspects and unhappy with the bad aspects of any decision I make. I don't have to pretend that everything is perfect just because I chose that particular path."*

Positive Power is the power to live life fully — the power to be human and the power to be you. You can use the Positive Power tapes that you have seen in these pages and you can generate your own as well. To make up Positive Power tapes, just follow these simple rules:

1) Use the word "I," as in, "I can do it."

2) Make the message positive, as in, "I can be happy."

3) Allow for imperfection, as in, "It's okay to be wrong."

Good luck!

2
Understanding Parents

PARENTS ARE UNUSUAL people. Other people are just people, but parents are *parents* — very special people with a very special impact on us. That is because we are little and helpless when we are born; we are totally dependent on our parents for our every need. As parents take care of us and raise us, we become very attached to them, very indebted to them, and greatly impressed by them. When we're small, parents seem to us to be perfect and all-powerful.

Of course, as we get older, we must always consider our parents to be distinguished[1] even as we start to notice that they are also normal people. They are not without human failings. Sometimes they have problems. Sometimes they lose their patience. Sometimes they say something hurtful. Sometimes they behave exactly the way they ask us not to!

No matter what parents do, however, the Torah demands of Jewish children a certain standard of behavior. Young people cannot simply vent their frustrations in a disrespectful manner. This harms them, even more than it harms their parents! When a Jewish son or daughter knows how to interact with parents properly, he or she reaps enormous benefits and reaches a high level of personal perfection.[2] Moreover, the laws of honor and respect for one's parents also provide the best techniques for effective and successful communication. In other words, young people will have a better relationship with their parents if they know how to express themselves in the right way.

Understanding why parents behave as they do is important to the process of getting along with them: you are more able to respond and behave in positive ways when you know what your parents want. Understanding your own reactions to your parents is also essential to the process of creating harmony.

One thing to know, for example, is that even the everyday behavior of parents can affect you in unusual ways. For example, if a friend of yours told you that your hair always looks messy, you might feel hurt for a couple of minutes and then get over it by telling yourself that what she says doesn't matter. However, if your *mother* made the very same comment (particularly if she made it often), you might feel bad about your hair for the rest of your life! Your mother's opinion and your father's opinion are more important to you than anyone else's.

We can see, then, that the ordinary things that parents say can actually have life-long effects on their children. But this can sometimes lead to problems. Parents don't necessarily intend their every comment to have lasting meaning. For example, a tired mother who impatiently tells a child he is careless certainly does not want him to think of himself as a careless person for the rest of his life! Because parents don't always use perfect techniques of communication, they themselves can cause misunderstandings. Also, children, because of their age or inexperience, can often misunderstand their parents. For instance, a son can think that his father is angry at him when this isn't true at all. Here's an example of a serious misunderstanding that happened to Ben as he was growing up.

Ben:
My father was always very cold and distant with me. He never joked around. He never seemed to have time for me. He was always very busy with his work, with shul, with learning, with community work. In fact, the only time he spent with me was at shul on Shabbos (where we couldn't talk) or at home reviewing what I learned in school (which was usually a tense time — especially if I didn't know my stuff). I felt that he didn't really like me. I was pretty sure he didn't love me. Inside, I was really hurt.

So you can imagine my shock when the day came that my father told me how much he always loved me and what a great son I'd been. It was the eve of my departure for an out-of-town yeshivah. Father was saying goodbye and wishing me success in my studies. That much I expected. But I was totally unprepared for his emotional leave-taking. Tears actually came to his eyes as he hugged me and told me how proud he was of me. I wondered, then, if he'd always felt that way but just never showed it.

Indeed, almost all parents love their children. However, many do not successfully convey their love. In other words, the parents love their child but the child does not know that this is so.

There are many reasons why a person may not succeed at showing his love. For example, Ben's father, Mr. Diamond, explains his own difficulty this way.

Mr. Diamond:

I always had a lot of trouble showing my feelings. My own father (may he rest in peace) died when I was only an infant. I was the youngest of four children, and the other three were quite a bit older than me. My mother was a poor widow working day and night to make ends meet — she had many worries and very little time for me. I guess I never had an opportunity to learn how one shows love.

As I was growing up, I kept to myself a lot. I threw myself into my studies, and later, into my work. I am very active in our community and that, combined with my busy schedule of working and learning, has left me with little time for my children. However, I have always loved them all.

In some cases, a parent doesn't show his love because he just never learned how to do so. He does not mean to cause his own children any pain; he simply knows no way of expressing himself. This tendency to pass a problem down through the generations can be seen in many other examples. For instance, Chaya describes her family's interactions.

Chaya:

My mother yells a lot. If I do anything wrong (like drop my schoolbag in the front hall instead of putting it away in the cupboard) she screams!

I often wish my mother would speak to me more quietly and calmly. But I think I know why she shouts: she told me how Bubby always shouted at her when she was young! I guess she copied what she saw at home. I'm going to try really hard to break the pattern, though. I really want to be a soft-spoken parent.

So your parents' behavior may be explained (although not excused) by *their* parents' behavior. Understanding this can help to remove some of the pain you might feel during an unpleasant conversation. Also, it frees you up to "translate" your parents' words into other words that are more pleasant and that probably reflect their true feelings more accurately. For instance, Sarah came in half-an-hour late one evening to this greeting.

Sarah's Mother:
HOW DARE YOU COME HOME AT THIS TIME OF NIGHT! YOU'RE GROUNDED FOR A MONTH FOR THIS!

At first, Sarah was quite upset by her mother's words. The shouting distressed her; the punishment depressed her. However, later on that evening, when Sarah calmed down, she thought about her mother's reaction some more. She realized that it was, deep down, an expression of her mother's concern for her. So she translated her mother's message in her own mind this way.

Sarah's Translation:
I was so worried about you! I love you so much and I thought maybe something terrible happened to you! Please don't scare me like that again!

Having made this translation, Sarah felt sorry that she had upset her mother, and she was no longer quite as angry at her mother for punishing her.

In fact, this is just an application of the Jewish law to judge a person favorably. We feel better ourselves when we judge someone favorably.[3] By giving them the benefit of the doubt, we experience less resentment and more pleasure. And indeed, there is good reason to judge parents favorably, since most parents are not intentionally hurtful to their children. On the contrary, they sincerely love their children and want the best for them. Your parents are actually showing their love for you when they get upset by the things you do; if they didn't care about you, they wouldn't care about your behavior. Yes, they may hurt your feelings sometimes and this naturally disappoints you. However, you disappoint them sometimes as well. This doesn't stop them from loving you; don't stop loving them just because they don't always speak to you in the way you'd prefer.

It sometimes happens, once in a long while, that a parent is truly abusive to his children. It is impossible to do a "translation" because the parent seems really to want to hurt his child. In that case, the child should turn to his rabbi, school principal, or guidance counselor for help or a referral to a professional counselor.

WHEN PARENTS CRITICIZE

One of the things that parents often do is criticize their children. "Stop annoying your sister." "Your room is a mess!" "Your hair needs washing." "You're lazy (selfish, inconsiderate, thoughtless, etc.)" "You waste your time." "You never help out."

Comments like these hurt. You sometimes begin to wonder if it's all true: you start to feel like a bad person or a stupid or ugly one. You may start to develop Bad Judge tapes in your mind which say things like, "i'm no good." "Nobody loves me." "i'm worthless." "i'll never succeed."

But parents don't want you to feel worthless. They criticize you because they want you to become the best person you can be. Indeed, it is the obligation of parents to correct their children in order to set them on the right path.[4] Without correction, we might all be forever hoarding our belongings, wetting our diapers, and eating with our hands! The trouble that our parents take to correct us results in our ability to be educated, sophisticated, normal people.

Like all medicine, correction must be given in carefully controlled doses. Criticism doesn't work well unless employed with extreme sensitivity.[5] When done too frequently, too harshly, or without regard for the feelings of the recipient, criticism does not provide the education it was meant to provide. Indeed, when a person is hurt by criticism, he begins to doubt himself. When he doubts himself, he doesn't perform as well as he actually can. Thus a person who lives with too much criticism ends up functioning less well and less happily than one who is subject to a more moderate, buffered amount.

If you live with very critical parents, you may have to work hard to replace your Bad Judge tapes with positive ones. You have to learn to think the thoughts that will give you encouragement and optimism. This hard work is a true personal accomplishment, worth every bit of the effort involved. Moreover it is an enormous credit to those who rise to the challenge. In addition to erasing your own negative programming, you can also learn some strategies to help your parents educate you without criticizing you excessively or destructively. For example, read these two dialogues.

Wrong Way:

Miriam: "I've got nothing to do today!"

Mother: "Miriam, you never make arrangements to do things with people on Sunday afternoon. No wonder you don't have any friends."

Miriam: "That's not true. I call people plenty of times but everyone's always busy."

Mother: "That's because you wait till the last minute — you never plan ahead."

Miriam: "If I call on Thursday, no one knows what they're doing yet. There's no point in calling before Sunday morning."

Mother: "You just don't know how to go about it."

Miriam: "It's not true! Last Thursday I asked Rachel to come over on Sunday and by the time Sunday came she was in bed with the flu."

Mother: "Well things like that happen occasionally. You can't refuse to make plans just because they won't always work out. That's not a mature attitude."

Miriam: "You don't like the way I do anything!"

Right Way:

Miriam: "I don't have anything to do today!"

Mother: "Miriam, you never make arrangements to do things with people on Sunday afternoon. No wonder you don't have any friends."

Miriam: "*Mommy, it hurts my feelings when you say I don't have friends.*"

Mother: "*Well, I just mean that you'd have more friends if you remembered to call people up.*"

Miriam: "*Thanks for the suggestion, Mommy.*"

In the wrong dialogue we see that Miriam works hard to defend and explain herself. However, every retort of hers brings more criticism from her mother. In the right dialogue, Miriam *tells her mother how her words make her feel*: she lets her mother know that her criticism hurts her feelings. This is always a good technique, one that may bring a quick end to further criticism. Mother doesn't really want to hurt her daughter's feelings — she's just trying to get a point across. Having been told that she's actually hurting her child, she will probably try to make her point again, in a way that is not so hurtful. When the point is made nicely, Miriam *thanks her mother for the idea*. This signals the end of the conversation. If Miriam's mother would have tried to say more on the subject, Miriam could have continued to thank her. This technique usually calms people down and discourages them from being hurtful.

These strategies work well for the normal interactions with a normally critical parent. However, the young person who is subject to constant, unrelenting criticism may need additional strategies. After all, a person who is criticized from sunrise to sunset may be tempted to respond in a hostile fashion. Some young people have been known to scream at their parents or insult them when they feel they "can't take anymore." Such behaviors are completely forbidden according to Jewish law.[6] No matter what a parent says or does —

even if the parent is clearly violating Jewish law in his own behavior — a child (of any age) must respond respectfully.[7] There is no obligation to like what your parent has said — only an obligation to remain respectful in your response.

In fact, children are not allowed to argue with their parents or contradict them in any way (although when essential, it is permissible to question a parent's statement politely, using the format, "Father/Mother, is it possible that...?").[8] These laws are for your benefit. They help you to remain a refined person, free from arrogance and unpleasant personality traits. They prevent you from becoming obnoxious, haughty, ill-mannered, or otherwise objectionable. After all, every response you make is actually practicing for the kind of person you will eventually be. If you shout now, you are practicing shouting for the future. If you are abusive now, you are turning yourself into an abusive person. Therefore, no matter how much you don't like the way a parent criticizes you, you must be very careful about how you respond.

So how can you handle excessive criticism? One effective criticism-stopper is to *agree* with the criticism being made. Never use a sarcastic tone of voice. You can just say, "Okay," or "Yes," or "You're right." (You do not have to repeat the criticism, as in "Yes, I'm selfish.") These responses avoid defending and arguing, bringing the conversation to a quicker and more painless close.

Agreeing with your parent's criticism does not mean that you agree that you are a terrible person. It could very well be that every critical remark your parent makes is based on a true fault of yours — we all have numerous faults, and there is no need to pretend that we are anywhere near perfect. However, you, like everyone else, also do at least a hundred things right every day — probably more. Although your parent may not mention all these things that you do right, be sure to remind yourself of them, so that you will not feel defeated by acknowledging some of the things that may need improvement. For example, if Mother points out that you didn't sweep the floor properly, remind yourself that you *did* sweep the floor! Play lots of Positive Power tapes to counterbalance the criticism that you must respond to.

Another strategy is to *offer no response at all* in those circumstances which do not demand a reply. For example, if Mother says, "You never hang up your clothes," she is not asking you a question which demands an answer. It may be best not to say anything at all. Silence on your part will actually lessen your tendency to become angry. To retort is halachically wrong, builds your anger, and invites an unpleasant confrontation.

A third very important strategy to use if you live with hypercritical parents is to seek professional counseling. Your school principal, guidance counselor, or rabbi may be able to help you find the right help. Remember that seeing a counselor does not mean that you have emotional problems! A proper counselor can help *prevent* emotional problems from arising by showing you effective ways to deal with your feelings and with your parents. Your counselor may also be effective in helping your parents understand your needs as well.

Wrong Way:

> Mother: "Sarah, put your books away now please."
>
> Sarah: "I will just as soon as I finish reading this page."
>
> Mother: "Sarah, I asked you to do it now. You always tell me you'll do it later."
>
> Sarah: "I don't! I just want to finish the page I'm on!"
>
> Mother: "Don't contradict me! That's another thing — you always talk back to me and I'm getting good and tired of it."
>
> Sarah: "I'm not contradicting you! I said I'd put the books away! Can't I just finish reading one little page?"
>
> Mother: "No! Why can't you just do as you're asked for once?"

Right Way:

> Mother: "Sarah, put your books away now please."
>
> Sarah: "I will just as soon as I finish reading this page."
>
> Mother: "Sarah, I asked you to do it now. You always tell me you'll do it later."
>
> Sarah: "You're right."

Notice that in the "right" dialogue, the conversation is over as soon as Sarah agrees with her mother's criticism, whereas in the "wrong" dialogue, the criticisms go on and on with every defensive statement that Sarah makes.

Disrespect is prohibited by the Torah — and it also makes more problems. It never leads to more happiness or more successful relationships.

Techniques:

1) Tell your parent how his/her words make you feel.

2) Thank your parent for his/her suggestions.

3) Agree with parent.

4) Remain silent.

5) Seek counseling.

WHEN PARENTS SEEM TO MAKE EXCESSIVE DEMANDS

Sometimes parents seem to want a lot from their children. They want their youngsters to excel in school, have lots of friends, be capable and responsible around the house, and be happy almost all the time. Parents may also want their children to fulfil their own unfulfilled dreams — to become the student they never were, the popular person they never were, the wealthy person they never became, and so on.

However, young people — like their parents — are only human! Sometimes they get less than perfect scores on their tests (didn't this ever happen to you?), can't seem to find a friend, do housework in a careless and sloppy way, whine, mumble, pout, or otherwise do not demonstrate absolutely perfect behavior all the time.

Since parents want their children to be the best human beings possible, their goals are probably similar to your own. You also want to be an excellent human being! You probably would like to succeed academically, socially, and in every other way. You're probably doing the best you can toward that end. It can happen, however, that you think you're trying as hard as you can and yet your parents aren't satisfied. They seem to want more from you than you can give. Here's what can happen.

Wrong Way:

Mother: "Goldie, could you please give Eli a bath and put him to bed for me?"

Goldie: "Again? You ask me to do so much! Nobody I know has so much to do at home! I have to make the sandwiches, wash the dishes, bathe the baby, read him stories, take out the garbage — I barely have time to do my homework, let alone call my friends! I'm going to have a nervous breakdown!"

Right Way:

Mother: "Goldie, could you please give Eli a bath and put him to bed for me?"

Goldie: "Okay. By the way, Mommy, I'm finding that with all my chores I barely have time to do my homework, and I really don't have time to call friends or even relax a little. Do you think it's unreasonable for me to ask if we could lighten up my schedule a little?"

In the "wrong" dialogue, Goldie's hysterical response to her mother's request is forbidden according to Jewish law.[9] Like all wrong responses, it doesn't work well. It is most likely to make her mother quite upset, leading to an unpleasant scene. Instead of understanding Goldie, Mother might feel angry at her, and she will certainly consider her disrespectful. Moreover, because Goldie has been too dramatic and hostile, she has lowered her chances of getting a sympathetic hearing and a positive answer.

In the "right" dialogue, Goldie *speaks in such a respectful way* that it is very likely her mother will really *hear* what she has to say. By asking — instead of demanding — to revise her schedule, Goldie opens the door to negotiation. Moreover, she *starts off by saying "yes"* to her mother's request. This will put her mother in an agreeable frame of mind. Goldie *speaks in a calm tone of voice* instead of shrieking — another technique that will raise the chances of her getting the kind of response she is looking for.

Techniques:

1) Speak in a respectful manner.

2) Start off by agreeing.

3) Speak in a calm tone of voice.

WHEN PARENTS LIMIT YOU

Parents limit the behavior of their children. This is an important part of their job.[10] It is not easy or pleasant for them, but if they don't do it their children may not grow into healthy, happy, normal, or moral people.[11] It is actually a sign of how much they love their children that parents are willing to say no.[12] They must teach small children not to hurt each other, not to fight, not to steal, not to call names, not to lie, not to do dangerous things, not to whine and cry for attention, and so on. They must teach older children not to be self-centered, not to be materialistic, not to be irresponsible, not to be lazy, and much more.

Children, however, do not like to be limited. The little child who wants to be messy wants his parents to let him be messy. The bigger child who wants to read all kinds of books wants her parents to let her read all kinds of books.

Moreover, young people are in the process of experimenting with living. They want to try out different kinds of behaviors to see which ones suit them best. They don't like their parents to interfere with this experimentation. They don't like to hear the word "no" or to suffer consequences for noncompliance.

Nonetheless, as a young person, you will often be confronted with "no." What is the best way to handle a negative response? What should you say? What should you do? Here are some possibilities.

Wrong Way:

>   *Father: "Deena, your mother and I have a new rule for you to follow: no telephone calls until after your homework is completed."*
>
>   *Deena: "WHAT? WHY? You know I have to do my homework on the phone lots of times! How can I ever follow a rule like that?"*
>
>   *Father: "You'll just have to find a way. Your marks are slipping dangerously low, and we feel this will help you succeed."*
>
>   *Deena: "You're so mean! You're not being fair — no one has a rule like that. By the time I'm finished with*

my schoolwork it'll be too late to call anybody. I won't have any friends left!"

Father: "Well I guess that's too bad, but that's just how it's going to be until we see some improved grades from you, young lady."

Right Way:

Father: "Deena, your mother and I have a new rule for you to follow: no telephone calls until after you've completed your homework."

Deena: "Oh. You want me to do my homework before talking on the phone. Would it be possible for you to explain the reason for the new rule?"

Father: "Certainly. Your marks have been slipping dangerously low, and we feel that this rule will remedy that problem and help you to succeed."

Deena: "You feel that my low marks are due to my speaking on the phone. I understand that you could think that, but I can explain myself. I use the phone for studying lots of times — it actually helps me with my schoolwork. Are you saying that I shouldn't do that anymore? Also, if I start my homework after supper — say, around seven o'clock by the time I finish helping with the dishes — I won't be finished with my work till ten on most nights. Since my friends aren't usually allowed to speak on the phone after ten at night, I'm afraid I wouldn't be able to speak to anyone anymore with the new rule."

Father: "Well what time at night do YOU think you

should be starting and finishing your schoolwork?"

Deena: "I never have more than three hours of homework, so if I started at eight o'clock, I could be finished by eleven at the latest. Would it be all right if I talked on the phone before eight, provided that I worked on my homework without interruptions from that point on?"

Father: "I'll discuss it with Mommy, but it sounds all right to me. We could probably give it a try and see how things go. I'll let you know later tonight."

Again, we find in the "wrong" dialogue that a hysterical response does not get the best results. Deena's outburst just puts her father on edge, and her outright disrespect (name-calling — a serious violation of Jewish law!)[13] puts his back up. When Deena tells her father that he is unfair and calls him "mean," she is using "you-messages." These are statements which complain about another person. The complainer is saying there is something the matter with "you." This usually puts the other person on the defensive and can make him angry. In fact, Deena's father becomes more rigid in response to her tirade.

In the "right" dialogue, Deena gets her point across — she doesn't want be cut off from her friends, and she thinks she has an idea which will permit her both to use the phone and improve her grades. Since she doesn't shriek or exaggerate her feelings, her father does not get defensive. He hears her concern and helps her to deal with it. Deena's calm and respectful interaction permits her father to take her suggestions seriously. Deena and her father keep their good feelings about each other, and they manage to solve their problem at the same time.

Deena uses two important techniques in this conversation. The first one is that *she lets her father know that she understands what he is saying.* (For example, she says, "Oh. You want me to do my homework before talking on the phone.") This is called giving "feedback." Feedback lets a person know that you heard what he said. Deena gives her father feedback even before she tells him her problem. This makes Deena's father feel that his daughter is receiving his message. This is a good feeling which increases the chances that he will try to help her.

The second technique is that *she tells him her own worries in a calm way.* When Deena explains her problem, she uses an "I-message." This is a statement of her own feelings, as in "I feel really uncomfortable (happy, sad, disappointed, frustrated, etc.)." I-messages make people feel sympathetic to your problems rather than defensive about them.

These techniques can be applied to most "limit" problems. For example, suppose your mother doesn't want you to attend a sleepover party on a school night, but your friends all plan on going. You can say, "Mommy, I know you don't think that I should go to bed so late during the week, but all my friends will be there. I feel so different from everyone. It's an awful feeling." Or, if your parents say you can't go to an expensive restaurant with your pals but all your classmates are going, you can say, "I know how you feel about the restaurant, and I see your point. But where does that leave me? I feel all alone." Or, if your mother thinks you want too many new outfits, you can say, "I understand that you think I've got enough to wear, but all the kids in my class are getting new things for Yom Tov. I feel really out of it with my usual outfits. I mean, I feel like people are laughing at me or, even worse, pitying me. Do you have any suggestions for me? Is there any way I can be 'in' without going against your wishes?"

These kinds of statements awaken memories that your parents have of being different and alone. They remember when they felt this way and it wasn't pleasant. They are therefore more likely to try to help you to do the right thing in such a way that you won't have to suffer unduly. Instead of being on opposite sides of the fence, you and your parents can work together to meet both your needs. Of course, a child is obligated to obey his parents whether or not he likes their decisions.[14] However, by speaking respectfully to parents, you increase the chances that they will try to make decisions that you will be happy to accept.

Techniques:

1) Give feedback first. (Let your parents know you heard and understood their statement.)

2) Use I-messages. (Describe your own feelings.)

3) Don't use you-messages. (Avoid statements about what is wrong with the person you are speaking to.)

WHEN PARENTS DON'T UNDERSTAND YOU

Often parents don't understand their children. This can happen because busy parents can't always take the time to listen carefully. It can happen because some parents lack good listening skills. It can happen because some children don't have good communication skills. Whatever the reason, it can be very frustrating when it happens to you.

Here's an example of being misunderstood. See how Tova handles it.

Wrong Way:

> *Mother: "The principal from the seminary will be in town next week, and I've made an appointment for you to meet with him."*
>
> *Tova: "But Mommy, I told you I don't want to go to school out of town."*
>
> *Mother: "Don't be ridiculous. Almost your whole class is going out of town. There's no point in you staying here."*
>
> *Tova: "I don't care. I don't want to go."*
>
> *Mother: "You'll love it once you're there."*
>
> *Tova (shouting): "I'M NOT GOING!"*
>
> *Mother: "Yes you are. And your appointment is Tuesday at three o'clock, so be ready for it."*

Right Way:

> *Mother: "The principal from seminary will be in town next week, and I've made an appointment for you to meet him."*
>
> *Tova: "You made an appointment? But Mommy, do you remember that I told you that I don't want to go to school out of town?"*

> Mother: *"Don't be ridiculous. Almost your whole class is going out of town. There's no point in you staying here."*
>
> Tova: *"I know most of the girls are leaving, but I just don't feel ready to leave home. I like being here."*
>
> Mother: *"You'll love it once you're there."*
>
> Tova: *"I'm sure you're right, but what do I do about my feelings right now? I just don't feel ready to leave home. I'm scared. Do you understand what I mean?"*
>
> Mother: *"Sure I understand. You're scared. That's natural — you've never been away from home. Maybe we can do something to help you be less scared."*

In the "wrong" example, Tova's mother is talking without really listening to her daughter. However, Tova is doing nothing to help the situation. She only repeats one thought over and over — she doesn't explain herself or try to help her mother to understand her better. Realizing that her mother doesn't understand, Tova tries speaking louder (she shouts), not realizing that louder voices usually stop any kind of understanding from taking place.[15] Both Tova and her mother are contributing to their poor communication.

In the "right" example, Tova takes steps to help her mother understand her better. First of all, she *explains her point of view*. Instead of just saying, "I don't want to go," she gives a reason: "I don't feel ready to leave home." She doesn't wait for her mother to ask her to explain — she just does it.

Second, to help her mother respond to her concern, Tova *asks her for feedback* by saying, "Do you understand what I mean?" This helps her mother to respond to her last statement and the conversation can move along.

Third, Tova speaks in a *normal tone of voice* while trying to explain her concerns. This increases the chances that her mother will listen to her with "open ears." In addition, Tova *gives her mother feedback* by saying again what her mother said, showing her mother that she heard and understood her.

In the "right" dialogue, Tova and her mother are communicating. Tova's mother will soon understand what her daughter is feeling and thinking because her daughter is helping her. Moreover, she will want to try to create a solution that will be satisfying to both of them.

It is possible that Tova's mother might have done a better "listening job" on her own if this conversation were taking place at a different moment in time. Although she initiated the conversation by pointing out that Tova had an appointment, she might have said this in passing as she was in the middle of baking, and then felt frustrated about trying to concentrate on two things at once. Even if she wasn't actually physically occupied with some task, she might have had a hard day with many pressing concerns and was in no frame of mind to have a pleasant, reasonable discussion. Tova could have been on the alert for such possibilities and gently offered to talk about the subject a little later on or perhaps tomorrow. Certainly, timing is important whenever listening is important. Both parties to a conversation need to be in a relaxed, positive frame of mind if real communication is to occur. Therefore, if a conversation doesn't seem to be going well, consider trying to have it again at another, better time.

Techniques:

1) Explain your point of view. Give as much information as you can about your thoughts and feelings. This will help your parent to understand you.

2) Ask for feedback. Check to make sure your parent heard and understood your last statement or idea.

3) Always explain your point of view calmly, without whining, shouting, or crying.

4) Give feedback by repeating what your parent has said to you as each new statement is made.

5) Consider the timing. Try again later if necessary.

GETTING ALONG WITH PARENTS

As mentioned earlier, parents are actually people. This means that they have feelings like you do. They sometimes get disappointed, frustrated, upset, tired, embarrassed, confused, scared, and worried. They can also feel happy, excited, relaxed, confident, silly, proud, and relieved. They enjoy getting along with people and they dislike fighting with people — just like you do. And they need lots of love, encouragement, and support — just like you do!

Parents, like all other people, respond well to "positive strokes." Positive strokes are words and actions that feel pleasant. For example, here are some positive strokes that you can give your parents:

- smiles
- kisses
- words of praise ("Mom, that was a great dinner!")
- words of gratitude ("Thanks, Mom.")
- small gifts
- love notes and memos ("You're the best father in the world!")
- listening and responding
- talking (sharing experiences, ideas, feelings)
- doing activities together (working, shopping, cooking)
- complying with a request
- helping
- serving (bringing food and drinks, carrying parcels)

Positive strokes like these feel good to parents. You want to make your parents happy — and that's only fair, considering all they do for you. But giving "positive strokes" is beneficial not only for your parents — it's good for you as well. If you give your parents a lot of positive strokes, they will most likely feel good being around you and will be happy to do things with and for you. On the other hand, if you give your parents lots of "negative strokes" instead, not only are you showing ingratitude, you will also find that your parents feel tense and uncomfortable around you and are less inclined to understand your point of view.

Negative strokes are words and actions that feel unpleasant. They are clear-cut violations of Jewish law.[16] Here are some examples of negative strokes:

- frowns, snarls, and other grouchy faces
- angry tone of voice (including yelling)

- criticism ("You never let me do anything I want to do!")
- complaints ("Why can't you make another kind of dinner?")
- insults ("Your handwriting is too messy.")
- whining, begging, and crying
- demanding and making repeated requests
- ignoring
- slamming doors
- disobeying or refusing to comply with a request
- stamping foot
- throwing or destroying things

You can improve the chances that your parents will get along with you by increasing your use of positive strokes in all aspects of your life. You should aim to make the majority of the things you say and do positive strokes.

For example, in the morning before you leave to school you could greet your mother with a cheery "Good morning Mom!" This will make Mother feel relaxed and happy. On the other hand, you could get up in the morning sounding something like this:

"MOMMY! TELL RONI TO STAY OUT OF MY DRAWERS: HE LOST MY BEST PEN!...What's for breakfast? Can't we get anything to eat besides plain old cereal? There's nothing to eat here.... MA! RISA TOOK MY BRUSH AND I NEED IT RIGHT NOW!...Why do I have to clean up after the baby? I'm in a big rush, you know, and nobody else has to do anything except me...."

By the time you're ready to leave, Mother feels drained, tense, and upset.

Clearly, a pleasant smile and gracious manner will go a long way towards creating a warm, happy atmosphere at home. On the other hand, an onslaught of negative strokes — a grouchy face and irritable tone of voice — makes for a tense, upset household.

Even if your parents give lots of negative strokes, you can begin to turn things around by using more positive strokes yourself and ignoring a lot of their negative strokes. Using mostly positive strokes will help you to get along best with your parents and help your parents to get along best with you. It won't solve every difficulty and it won't make everything work out perfectly — but it will sure help a lot. Try it and see!

INSTEAD OF HEADACHES

Parents are people. This means that, like you, they are capable of making mistakes. Sometimes, however, parents don't even realize that they're making a mistake. For example, a parent may accidently punish a child too harshly for some minor infraction. In response, the respectful child who does not dare rebel may "get a headache" — may swallow feelings of outrage or despair, making himself sick in the process. In fact, whenever feelings are suppressed, there is the possibility of getting physically sick. Unresolved frustration, anger, grief, or any other negative emotion can end up bothering you in the form of headaches, stomach aches, asthma, and any number of other physical ailments, because unexpressed feelings can never disappear; they simply get rerouted within the body.

In order to avoid getting sick in this way, it is essential to learn to express your feelings to your parents. Providing you are always respectful in your speech, there is no problem with asking your parents to consider your concerns. Look at this scenario for example.

Wrong Way:

> *Mother:* "Miriam, I asked you to have the dishes washed by the time I got home, and I see you haven't even started them. You've just lost the use of the car for six months."
>
> *Rachel:* (Gets a headache.)

Right Way:

> *Mother:* "Miriam, I asked you to have the dishes washed by the time I got home, and I see you haven't even started them. You've just lost the use of the car for six months."
>
> *Rachel:* "Mom, I'm really sorry about the dishes. I didn't pay attention to the time. I can understand that you're upset — I don't blame you. Would you consider an alternative punishment? Maybe I could do the dishes every day for two weeks instead of losing the car for six months. And if I miss even one day, then we'll go back to the car punishment. Would you think about it?"
>
> *Mother:* "I'll think about it. I'll let you know tomorrow."

Actually, Rachel's mother is quite happy to be "let off the hook." She realized her punishment was excessive, but she didn't know how to get out of it without being inconsistent. Because Rachel raised the subject, Mother has an opportunity to reconsider. Best of all, Rachel does not have to just swallow her upset feelings. By expressing her concerns, she saves herself a headache.

If you feel that your parents have been too strict, inflexible, unfair, or unreasonable in some way, try to talk to them about it. No accusation is necessary — or permissible! A child is permitted to question a parent using a respectful format like, "Daddy, is it possible that...?"[17] Your question can be considered by your parent; it is not guaranteed that your parent will change his mind. However, you'll never know if he will or not unless you ask!

Young people can also get headaches from living with tense parents who don't express their feelings. Sometimes adults have problems of their own which create tension in the household: problems with harmony in the marriage, personal stresses, family stresses, financial stresses, health difficulties, or other issues. Struggling adults don't always want to talk openly about the challenges they are facing. This can leave children feeling alone and maybe even guilty. Young people need a warm, relaxed atmosphere in which to flourish; if that cannot be arranged, then good, open communication helps them to make the best adjustment to a difficult situation. Here's Leah's predicament.

Wrong Way:

> *Leah: "What's going on with Bubby? Is everything okay? There've been so many phone calls and everyone's running around. What's happening?"*
>
> *Mother: "I don't want to discuss it now."*
>
> *Leah: (Gets a headache.)*

Right Way:

> *Leah: "What's going on with Bubby? Is everything okay? There've been so many phone calls and everyone's running around. What's happening?"*
>
> *Mother: "I don't want to discuss it now."*
>
> *Leah: "Would it be possible for you to tell me later on tonight or tomorrow then? I feel worried. I can't concentrate on my schoolwork 'cause I'm wondering about it. Sometimes not knowing something can be worse than knowing something bad, if you know what I mean."*
>
> *Mother: "Okay, sweetheart. We'll talk later."*

In the wrong dialogue, Leah keeps her frustration to herself, where it goes "underground" into the muscles of her head. In the right dialogue, Leah *expresses her feelings* appropriately. Some young people have to deal with very complex parental issues — issues like death, divorce, and remarriage, for example. Again, open communication of feelings will keep you functioning at your best through all such challenges. Even if your parents don't seem able or willing to discuss things with you, try to initiate respectful discussions about the issues that concern you.

Of course, parents aren't the only ones you can turn to. If you have a trusted advisor such as a favorite teacher, neighbor, rabbi, counselor, or a good friend, you can express yourself to that person as well. The important thing is to be able to get the guidance and support you are entitled to. Just having the opportunity to talk about your feelings can be powerful preventative medicine — preventing lots of headaches!

Understanding Parents

Techniques:

1) Express your concerns out loud to your parents.

2) Express your concerns to a trusted advisor.

As you can see, getting along with parents requires excellent communication skills on your part — the ability to express your needs and feelings with the utmost respect. However, once you master this ability, you will have developed a skill which will serve you well in all of your relationships in life. After all, knowing how to conduct yourself in a humble, respectful manner — as is demanded in the child-parent relationship — will make you a terrific friend, sibling, employee, colleague, boss, and marriage partner too!

Everyone appreciates being treated with respect. Everyone responds best to this kind of treatment. Because you know how to speak in a polite and respectful manner, everyone you interact with will be more cooperative and willing to please you. Because you can accept the human weaknesses of people while maintaining the utmost respect for them, all of your relationships will be successful. Most important, the life-long relationship you have with your parents will be the best it can be. So learn and practice these skills: see how they affect your life.

3
Understanding Siblings

HOW DO YOU get along with your siblings (brothers and sisters)? Do you love them (deep down) but find that you argue a lot with them? Maybe you get along with some of them and don't get along with others. Maybe, if you're one of the oldest, you sometimes find the younger ones to be a nuisance or a burden. And if you're a younger one, perhaps you sometimes find the older ones too bossy or too busy.

Although people can have a great relationship with one or more of their siblings, most people have some kind of complaint about their brothers and sisters at some point in time. Some people feel that one or more of their siblings are favored by their parents. Some feel that one or more of their siblings are so outstanding that they're hard to live up to. Some feel that one or more of their siblings are embarrassing for one reason or another. Some find some of their siblings hard to understand or relate to.

A very common feeling to have toward one's siblings is annoyance — because siblings can be so annoying! They may take your belongings without permission; they may damage what they borrow; they may intrude on your privacy; they may demand space, food, telephone time, and other resources that you don't want to share so much; they may hurt you physically in anger or in jest; they may insult you, make fun of you, and otherwise make you feel awful.

Of course, that's not to say that siblings don't have their good side. Siblings can be very helpful and caring. They may take you places, teach you things, keep you company when you're lonesome, pamper you when you're sick, cheer you up when you're sad, buy you gifts, defend you when necessary, do activities with you, and trade chores with you. If you're lucky, you'll have some siblings that really get along well with you and who will function like built-in best friends.

Although siblings are like other people you will encounter in your life (i.e., some will be compatible with you and some won't), they have an unusual characteristic in common with your parents: siblings are people whom you are forced to live with all through your growing-up years. When you get married to someone, you *choose* to live with that person. Moreover, you pick a person who you think will be easy for you to get along with, someone who's like you in a lot of ways, someone whose personality you'll enjoy. But siblings are people whom you *have* to live with whether you are compatible or not. You don't get to choose each other in advance. Perhaps you will have something in common with one or more of them. Perhaps the only thing you'll have in common with some of them is your parents!

Contrary to popular opinion, it is not necessary to be

best friends with each of your siblings. Of course, it would be fantastic if you all got along well and really enjoyed each other. Life would be so pleasant for all of you. The truth is, however, that very few people get along with *anyone* that well, whether that person is related or not related. Sure, you'll occasionally meet someone with whom you "click." You may have so much in common that you immediately understand each other and almost effortlessly get along. Nonetheless, even such natural bonds will require some amount of work in order to succeed. All relationships take work. Now, if you don't have that natural "click" to begin with, then more work will be required in order to build a harmonious relationship.

In fact, siblings provide excellent practice for the work of successful relationships. Siblings are always there. You can learn and practice the skills of getting along with people by testing them out on your own siblings. If you make mistakes, your siblings will still be there — they can't leave! And they can't get rid of you either! So you're stuck together in the ultimate trusting relationship (you can trust each other to be there), forced to work it through if you're going to live happily together. You can only quit working at it if you're willing to be unhappy — and few people are willing to settle for that!

When you've mastered the art of getting along with your siblings, you are truly prepared to have a successful relationship with anyone. You will be particularly well prepared to enter into a loving marriage relationship, because marriage requires a very similar give-and-take ability.

The art of getting along with siblings is really outlined

fully in the *Shulchan Aruch* (the Jewish code of law). In addition to the law of honoring one's older brother,[1] it basically involves following all of the laws that apply "man-to-man" — between a person and his fellow human being. It comes down to "loving your fellow man as yourself"[2] — treating others the way you'd like to be treated. This is what makes for good relationships. Let's look at some of these important skills for living successfully with siblings.

1. SAY IT WITH WORDS

Wrong Way:

> *Brother: (Grabs calculator out of his sister's hand, twisting her arm as he goes.)*

Right Way:

> *Brother: "Leah, please give me my calculator! I need it. Also, please ask me if you could use it before you take it from now on."*

Although it is fine to use body language to convey positive emotions (like smiling when you're pleased or hugging someone when you're feeling affectionate), it should never be used to communicate negative emotions. In other words, when you are unhappy about something, you should not try and tell someone about it by tripping him or sticking your tongue out at him. Such negative body language is an invitation to fight rather than an invitation to improve a situation. Instead, use words to explain your feelings and to ask for what you want. You will have a much greater likelihood of succeeding and of maintaining peaceful, happy relationships.

The greater success rate of words over body language is due to several factors. For one thing, body language is not always clear. Why is Leah's brother grabbing the calculator in the above example? Does he need it right away and lacks the courtesy to ask for it? Is he mad at his sister about something and is therefore being harsh in his treatment of her? Does he just want to torment her for fun? There's no way for her to be sure of what he is trying to say unless he actually says it with words. Moreover, the use of body language to engage in hurtful physical interactions, such as grabbing, hitting, kicking, and so on, destroys peace between people and hurts their feelings.

"Body language" also includes the use of facial expressions. For example, a person might just make a "face" in response to someone. Again the question will arise, "What does that face mean?" One can only guess: body language is much more ambiguous than verbal expression. If that face is an unpleasant one, it will also transgress the Torah prohibition against hurting others' feelings,[3] and of course, it will lessen the chances of having a peaceful interaction.

In the case of negative feelings like anger, disappointment, or fear, it is best to just say what you're feeling rather than trying to show it without words. Use I-messages which give a description of your feeling (e.g., "I'm really upset") instead of you-messages (e.g., "You make me really mad"). I-messages are more likely to be heard. Those accusing statements about "you" are likely to be rejected by the listener, and defended against. They often lead to a "fight" rather than a straightforward communication.

2. USE A NORMAL TONE OF VOICE

Wrong Way:

> *Sister (whining):* "Aviva, can't you finish with the phone already? I need it!"

Right Way:

> *Sister (pleasant tone of voice):* "Aviva, I need the phone. Could you possibly finish with it soon?"

When people hear an unpleasant tone of voice (shouting, whining, screeching, moaning, or whatever), they instinctively tense up. Instead of being open to what the speaker is saying, they fall into an uncooperative mood. How do *you* feel when someone shouts or whines at *you*?

If using an unpleasant tone of voice is such an unsuccessful strategy, why do so many people do it? Actually, it's no more than a bad habit learned in very early childhood. Children under the age of five or so often find that they can get what they want from their mothers if they make themselves obnoxious enough. For example, a child who asks his mother for a cookie may receive the answer, "No." Then the child make take to pleading, raising his voice, asking over and over, and using other assorted techniques — until his mother can no longer bear it and gives in to his demand. The child learns in this way that certain tones of voice may be useful for getting what he wants in this world.

The only problem is that what works on Mommy when you're three years old will not necessarily work well on other people (including brothers and sisters) when you are older. It certainly does not tend to work well on friends or marriage partners!

One particular tone of voice — the angry tone — is especially problematic in relationships. People sometimes shout instead of speaking quietly because they think that a more dramatic show of emotions will get more attention and better results. Although they are right about the attention part (usually people *notice* a message which is shouted at them), they are wrong about the results part. Shouting gets worse results — not better! When people try to solve problems loudly, their emotions get in the way. Hysteria is not conducive to clear thinking and good problem-solving. In addition, an angry state of mind leads one to say and do foolish and destructive things.[4] Instead of solving problems, you may end up hurting someone (which in itself is wrong, as we have previously seen)[5] and destroying your own happiness at home.[6] Shouting tends to increase one's feelings of anger (you get "worked up") and therefore decreases one's ability to negotiate problems properly.

If you find that you are so angry that you feel like shouting at your brother or sister, this is a signal for you to *refuse to discuss the bothersome subject at all.* Wait until you have calmed down. This might be minutes, hours, or days later. Only when you are calm enough to speak in a normal tone of voice should you raise the subject again.

For example, if your brother returns your favorite book to you in poor condition, you might feel like screaming, "WHAT DID YOU DO TO THIS BOOK?!!" However, if you really want him to be more careful with your possessions, you should wait until you're feeling calm enough to talk to him rationally. At that point you could tell him how upset you were to receive the book in that condition, and you might add quietly that you won't be inclined to lend him anything in the near future until he proves himself in some way, promises to pay for damages or replacement, or offers some ideas of his own that you find acceptable.

It's important, then, to experiment with new strategies in order to have successful grown-up relationships. Whining and shouting won't win you any friends — quite the contrary — so try something else. Since most people respond well to direct questions or statements spoken in a pleasant, normal tone of voice, you'll probably find that you get what you want more often by using this technique.

3. DON'T LABEL OR NAME-CALL

Wrong Way:

> *Rachel: "Why are you wearing my sweater?"*
>
> *Esther: "You said I could borrow it whenever I wanted."*
>
> *Rachel: "LIAR! I said you could ASK me permission to wear it whenever you wanted!"*

Right Way:

> *Rachel: "Why are you wearing my sweater?"*
>
> *Esther: "You said I could borrow it whenever I wanted."*
>
> *Rachel: "I think you're mistaken. I remember saying you could ASK me permission to wear it whenever you wanted."*

Labels are descriptive words which seem to sum up a person's personality. Here is a list of some negative labels: lazy, selfish, inconsiderate, careless, stupid, mean, messy, stubborn, greedy, snobbish. Name-calling is the use of labels which are particularly nasty such as "slob," "liar," or "fatso." Labels and name-calling should *never* be used to describe anyone (including yourself!). In fact, name-calling is one of the most serious transgressions of Jewish law — one which has extremely severe negative consequences.[7]

If you use labels to describe the person you are talking to, you will ruin your conversation and possibly your relationship. People react very badly to being labeled or called names. They become quite unlikely to cooperate with you; instead, they may want to hurt or antagonize you.

If you are really disappointed in your sibling's behavior, you can certainly tell him. However, instead of generalizing about the behavior by using a label, be very specific and describe exactly what the sibling did wrong in that situation. For example, suppose Bryna's brother came into her room and tossed things all over while he was looking for something that he thought he'd left there. Bryna could easily complain to him that he was "inconsiderate and thoughtless" by behaving in that way. However, this would not encourage him to be more considerate and thoughtful in the future. Rather, he might respond with sarcasm or hostility toward her. Bryna will be more likely to help her brother respect her property if she describes her problem without the use of labels (e.g., "I was really upset to find things scattered all over my room after I had tidied it up"). Such a statement will more likely elicit a cooperative — perhaps even empathetic — response. Because it does not antagonize, it helps to preserve a pleasant, respectful relationship.

4. ACCEPT COMPLAINTS GRACIOUSLY

Wrong Way:

> *Esther: "Rachel, stand up a little straighter. Your posture is terrible. You're always bent over!"*
>
> *Rachel: "You should talk! Your shoulders are so rounded that your sweaters fall off!"*

Right Way:

> *Esther: "Rachel, stand up a little straighter. Your posture is terrible. You're always bent over!"*
>
> *Rachel: "Really? How should I stand?"*

It is always a little difficult to accept criticism. Many people, especially young people, consider criticism to be a threat to their self-worth. However, there really is no threat. If the criticism is untrue (e.g., someone says that you are selfish and you are not selfish), then the critic himself has a problem — not you. And if the criticism is true (e.g., someone says you are selfish, and you do have a tendency to be selfish in some ways, even if not in the exact way that the critic means it), then it can help you to develop yourself — and this is a bonus for you. Every person can work on improving himself until the day he dies. None of us is perfect. The more we work on ourselves, the more we can reach our total human potential. In fact, the Torah teaches us to consider honest criticism as a wonderful and loving gift because it can help us to improve ourselves![8]

Therefore, when a sibling offers criticism, think twice before responding to it. Remember, family members know you better than anyone in the world. You can't "fake it" at home. Your siblings probably see you every day and share living quarters with you. If they say something about your behavior, they most likely have a point. They may be exaggerating this point, but there's probably at least an element of truth to what they are saying. Peel away the exaggeration and look at the kernel. Is there anything that you can work on? Don't be afraid; you can change your behavior. Thank the person who offers you advice. *Never retort with a criticism of your own!*

Of course, siblings (like other people) sometimes lack finesse. They may offer criticism in a hurtful way. They may use all kinds of improper and destructive techniques such as labeling, insulting, poking fun, exaggerating, belittling, embarrassing, and so on (all of which are very wrong). For example, a sibling might say something like:

"Hey, Fatso, have you considered going on a diet lately? You look like you could lose a hundred pounds around the waist alone!"

What's the best kind of response to criticism offered in such a style? Check off the replies below that you think would be appropriate:

__ 1. "Thanks for the advice."

__ 2. "Well, I don't want to get too skinny. People might confuse me with you."

__ 3. "Compliments won't get you anywhere."

___ 4. "I appreciate your concern."

___ 5. "You may not believe this, but I do have feelings and you are hurting them right now."

___ 6. "I guess we both have to work on our mouths — me in my way and you in yours."

___ 7. "I'm sure you're trying to be helpful but you could improve your effectiveness if you read this book of mine on communication skills — I'll be glad to lend it to you."

___ 8. "Why don't you shut your big mouth?"

___ 9. "All I have to do to look good is lose a few pounds — but NOTHING will help you!"

___ 10. "I may be fat but at least I'm not disgusting like some people I know."

If you put a check mark on any of the numbers from 1 to 7, you're on the right track. Some of those comments completely ignore the unfair and plain wrong elements of the criticism. Some of them give an honest, unhurtful statement of feelings. Some ignore the remark with the use of humor. (It isn't always necessary to respond to an insult, even if there is an element of truth in the remark. In fact, walking away without saying anything at all is an appropriate response.)

However, statements 8 to 10 are all retorts which are just as destructive and hurtful as the sibling's original criticism. They are transgressions in their own right. Natural as it is to try and hurt back when we are hurt, we must remember that we hurt *ourselves* by lowering ourselves to that kind of behavior. Why make ourselves disgusting just because someone acted in a disgusting manner toward us?

Is it worth it? Does it help our relationships? Does it bring us greater happiness? No! In fact, we end up liking ourselves less when we allow ourselves to act in unlikable ways. Therefore, if a sibling makes an unkind remark, always try to respond in the kindest way possible (humor usually helps). It'll be good for both of you.

5. GIVE IN

Wrong Way:

> Aaron: "Hey, who said you could walk off with the scissors? I was in the middle of using them!"
>
> Michel: "They were just lying on the counter so I picked them up — how was I supposed to know you were using them?"
>
> Aaron: "It was obvious! Anyone could see that I was cutting that string for Mom. Don't you have eyes in your head?"
>
> Michel: "Don't you have brains in yours? Do you think that everyone stands around watching what you're doing all night? I just came in now. How was I supposed to know what you're up to?"

Right Way:

> Aaron: "Hey, who said you could walk off with the scissors? I was in the middle of using them!"
>
> Michel: "Oh. Sorry. I didn't realize that."

Peace and harmony — the absence of fighting — is the

Understanding Siblings

ideal state in which to live. The Jewish way is to "seek peace and pursue it"![9] In other words, we are supposed to go out of our way to ensure that our interactions are peaceful ones. This is true not only with our friends and neighbors, but even more so with our family members.[10]

The person who develops the habit of apologizing easily has a powerful technique for maintaining peace. If someone accuses you of something, have a tendency to quickly say, "I'm sorry." It's possible to apologize even for things you didn't do in order to pursue peace: all the more should one learn to apologize for things one did accidentally, and certainly for those one did thoughtlessly or purposefully.

The habit of giving in is related to the habit of apologizing. "Better to be smart than to be right" is a saying applied to those who don't try to prove their "rightness" unnecessarily. The smart person keeps his interactions happy. The "right" person may win a few arguments, but loses in terms of contentment and satisfaction in life. Quarrelsomeness only brings tension and pain.[11] No one benefits from a quarrel — even the "right" person doesn't gain.

The person who knows how to apologize and give in is not a spineless wimp. In fact, this person is stronger than all others. "Who is strong? He who controls his evil inclination."[12] That is, he controls his anger and hostility and is able to accept his own errors calmly, without false defensiveness; therefore he is able to apologize when appropriate and he can "give in" instead of needing to preserve his honor on every occasion.

Moreover, when the issue really warrants it, a person in control of himself may not give in at all, but will defend his point. The question to be asked is, "is this point worth arguing about?" In ninety-nine percent of the cases, the answer will be "no." However, when the issue is of great importance, then is the time to explain or insist. At all other times, "giving in" is the best response, the one which will bring you the greatest happiness and the best relationships.

6. DO THINGS FOR YOUR SIBLINGS

Wrong Way:

> *Ruth: "Sarah, could you walk to school with me earlier this morning? I have some work to do before class starts but I don't want to go alone."*
>
> *Sarah: "I don't want to rush my breakfast."*
>
> *Ruth: "Please! I'd do it for you."*
>
> *Sarah: "Sure! Sure! Like the time I asked you to wait five minutes for me after school, and you were in such a big rush to go that you couldn't, and then I ended up getting home before you because you spent so long dawdling with your friends."*

Right Way:

> *Ruth: "Sarah, could you walk to school with me earlier this morning? I have some work to do before class starts but I don't want to go alone."*
>
> *Sarah: "Sure Ruth. Just let me grab a quick bite and I'll be right with you."*

Siblings are for life. Our most important relationships require our best efforts. That's why family mem-

Understanding Siblings

bers deserve our very best behavior — our kindest words and our most thoughtful actions. Certainly friends and neighbors deserve good treatment too, but some people make the mistake of treating other people better than they treat their own family. This is a bad habit to get into when you're young for it can easily carry over into your grown-up relationships, too. Imagine treating your marriage partner worse than you treat your neighbor! You can just picture how much unhappiness you would bring upon yourself.

Some people who don't get along well with their brothers and sisters during their youth later manage to establish warm adult relationships with them. By adulthood, many people have matured enough to know how to get along with people, including their own siblings! However, it happens just as often that siblings who didn't get along well when they were young, continue to interact poorly in later years. Moreover, those who were close when young tend to remain close in adulthood. Therefore, if you are hoping to have successful, loving, and close relationships with your brothers and sisters when you are all grown and married, the time to begin working on it is now.

In order to make your siblings into really good friends, treat them the way you would treat really good friends. If they don't live at home with you, call or write frequently. Visit often if you live near enough. If they live at home, talk to them (nicely). Offer to do things for them (bring them things, carry things, make them snacks, go places with them). Help them with homework, problems, chores. Take care of them when they're not feeling well. Listen to them when they need someone to talk to. Play games with them or learn with them or do crafts and hobbies with them. Buy or make them an occasional treat, in addition to celebrating birthdays or other important dates with them. In short, be kind, giving, and friendly. And don't wait for them to do all this for you — just put yourself out for them. Soon, they will reciprocate. Your siblings will appreciate and value your friendship long into the years ahead.

7. SAY NICE THINGS

Wrong Way:

> *Miriam: "You can't wear that dress this afternoon! It looks disgusting."*

Right Way:

> *Miriam: "Sarah, why don't you wear the blue dress this afternoon? It really looks gorgeous on you."*

Even siblings have feelings(!) and we are not allowed to hurt them.[13] Moreover, one who is careless about the feelings of his siblings is hardening himself, leading to the habit of being careless with the feelings of all people. So when we make ourselves insensitive to the feelings of our brothers and sisters, we eventually become insensitive to the feelings of everyone. We become people who aren't very nice.

The way to avoid this is to get in the habit of speaking kindly to our siblings. Kind words are words of praise (e.g., "Your handwriting is really neat") and words of encouragement (e.g., "Don't worry. Your speech will go really well, you'll see"). They are also words of appreciation (e.g., "Thanks for bringing the juice") and words of love (e.g., "You're a great sister!"). How often do you use these kinds of words with your siblings?

In addition to saying nice things, it is important *not to say* unkind things. Criticisms, unless very carefully worded, can be quite painful. This includes all complaints made to and about a sibling. It is true that you sometimes have a legitimate complaint to make, but it is not necessary to complain every time you have an opportunity. Learn to prioritize: select the most important complaints and mention those while deciding not to mention other complaints. Don't say everything that bugs you. Let things pass.

Again, this technique is an investment for the future — you'll make a much better spouse and parent if you master it! After all, you're not perfect either. We all should be allowed to make a few mistakes and do a few things wrong without constantly being picked on. And besides, no one makes friends by picking on people. In fact, that's a good way to lose friends. By increasing your tolerance level (allowing people to be human and do some things wrong), you will enjoy your siblings more. But not only that — you will actually enjoy everyone more and you will therefore enjoy life more! Try it and see.

8. SHARE POSSESSIONS

Wrong Way:

> *Tammy: "Leah, can I please borrow your hair dryer?"*
>
> *Leah: "No. It's mine and I don't want you to use it."*

Right Way:

> *Tammy: "Leah, can I please borrow your hair dryer?"*

Leah: "Okay, but please put it back in the cupboard when you're through with it."

It is an act of kindness and a mitzvah to lend our belongings, even minor ones such as combs and pencils.[14] People who borrow also have obligations — particularly to be careful not to damage what is borrowed.[15] However, siblings often feel possessive about their things to the point where they don't want to lend them to each other.

There are several reasons for this:

1) Past experience may have shown that shared items were often returned damaged or broken.

2) Past experience may have shown that shared items were returned late, at an inconvenient time, or not at all.

3) Past experience may have shown that shared items were permanently lost.

4) Certain possessions are very special and a person just doesn't want to lend them for that reason.

All of these are valid reasons for not wanting to lend belongings out. However, refusal to lend things is not only wrong but destructive. It is destructive because it ruins harmony in the home. Disappointed siblings can make quite a loud fuss when they are refused the item they wish to borrow. The whining, begging, screaming, or arguing which ensues is bad for the whole household (parents included), and particularly for the two people involved.

If sharing has been problematic in your home, it is possible to make it an easier and more comfortable experience by setting up a few household rules. For example, it can be stipulated that anyone who borrows an item must return it in good condition by an agreed-upon time or suffer an agreed-upon penalty. (E.g., Esther agrees to lend her red pen to Miriam provided that Miriam returns it by 7 p.m. Failure to return it by 7 will mean that Miriam has to do the dishes for Esther tomorrow, and failure to return it by the next day means that Miriam has to buy a new one for Esther.)

In addition, everyone in the family can have one item which he considers so special that it need not ever be loaned out. For example, David may have a baseball mitt which cost a lot of money that he worked hard to earn. Moreover, the mitt cannot be easily replaced because it was purchased out-of-town. Therefore, David can claim this item as the one which he will not lend out. However, the status of "special" can only be applied to that one item — he must be willing to lend out any of his other possessions provided the normal terms are agreed upon.

A third condition can be set up as well: anyone who doesn't cooperate with the penalty system (i.e., does not replace the object or does not abide by the penalty) will not be allowed to borrow anything for a three-month period. Repeated offenders can be penalized for a year or two!

It helps if all of these rules are suggested at a family meeting (at the dinner table is good, too) so that everyone in the house agrees to follow them. However, they can also be made as a private arrangement by any two or more siblings.

As usual, when you push yourself to be a cooperative and pleasant person — in this case, one who shares easily — you turn yourself into a better, more likeable human being. And *you* will like yourself just as much as everyone else will!

9. RESPECT THE PROPERTY OF YOUR SIBLINGS

Wrong Way:

> *Rachel: "Sarah, why are you wearing my sweater?"*
>
> *Sarah: "I found it on my bed — I thought you wouldn't mind."*
>
> *Rachel: "Well I do mind! I don't know how it got on your bed, but you have no right to just go ahead and wear it without asking me first!"*

Right Way:

> *Sarah: "Rachel, I found your sweater on my bed — do you mind if I wear it?"*
>
> *Rachel: "I don't mind as long as you're very careful with it — I don't want any stains on it or anything."*
>
> *Sarah: "Thanks, Rachel. Don't worry, if I wreck it I'll pay for repairs or replacement — but I'll be really careful with it so all that won't be necessary."*

Jewish law does not allow us to use someone else's possession without his permission, even if we intend to return it.[16] Doing so can easily aggravate a person. Many sibling fights begin just this way. Even though your brother or sister should share their things with you, you need to ask them for this privilege; never just take something without their express permission.

In the example above, Sarah happens to find her sister's sweater on her bed. Situations like this often occur in a household — people find pencils, pens, papers, money, clothing, toys, and all sorts of items in the wrong place. Often such items can even show up in your territory. Just because an article is not in its proper location does not mean that it is up for grabs. If you find a misplaced article that you would like to use, remember that that article has exactly the same status as it would have if it were in its proper place — it's not yours! You must ask permission to use it. Even if an item shows up in your drawer, it doesn't mean that someone put it there for you to use. More likely, it was a mistake that someone made and it shouldn't have been there at all.

Of course, the reason people sometimes don't ask if they can use something is because they expect a "no" answer. They'd rather just use the item and "face the music" later. Of course, this is totally wrong. Even if you do expect a "no" you should ask. In order to increase the chances of getting a positive reply you can offer to protect, repair, and replace the item if need be. You can also increase the likelihood of getting a "yes" if you yourself establish a track record of easy sharing. That is, if your siblings know they can count on you for a "yes" when they ask you for permission to use your things, they'll be much more likely to treat you the same way.

Related to the idea of respecting others' property is the concept of respecting their privacy. For example, one shouldn't read another person's mail without his permission because that would be an invasion of his privacy.[17] Similarly, one shouldn't enter a house (even his own) without knocking, so as not to suddenly intrude on anyone.[18] In fact, one shouldn't even enter someone's room without knocking. Siblings who are careful with each other's privacy in these ways are showing the kind of mutual respect which fosters excellent relationships. On the other hand, siblings who have the habit of barging in unannounced often find their reception less than warm; being the source of annoyance can only harm your relationships, thereby reducing your potential for happiness at home.

In order to enhance your sibling relationships, therefore, be careful to respect the privacy of everyone in your home: don't read others' correspondence; don't walk into their rooms without knocking; don't eavesdrop on their telephone conversations; don't insist on staying in the room when they are talking to other people. All of these precautions will earn you a good reputation at home and will also go a long way to ensuring that others will similarly respect your privacy!

10. SHARE SPACE

Wrong Way:

> *Leah: "Deena, get off my bed right now!"*
>
> *Deena: "What for? I'm not touching your stuff. I'm just sitting here."*
>
> *Leah: "Get off! I don't like you sitting on my bed and you know it."*

Right Way:

> *Leah: "Deena could you please move my books over a bit so your feet won't touch them when you're lying on my bed?"*
>
> *Deena: "Oh sure. Sorry, I didn't realize I was near them."*

Like sharing possessions, sharing space is a nice thing to do. Similarly, refusing to share space causes a lot of tension and aggravation between people who live together.

Some young people are quite "territorial." They treasure their private space. This is a natural tendency and even a healthy one, for it is all part of the process of becoming an individual. As we mature, we get more and more independent of others, more aware of our uniqueness and individuality. Because of this, we begin to define certain things as our own — not belonging to others. Once a thing has been so defined, we then set out to protect its borders and boundaries. This results in a feeling of possessiveness about belongings and space. We begin to feel that people shouldn't use our things or our usual spaces such as our rooms, beds, chairs, reading spots, or whatever.

Natural as it is, this feeling makes others uncomfortable. Therefore, a person must work on himself to overcome his possessiveness. As long as a sibling is not damaging your territory, let him use it whenever it is available. Again, you can set up conditions which will safeguard your interests: for example, you can arrange that a sister may sit on your bed whenever you are not sleeping in it, or a brother may use your desk provided he agrees to leave as soon as you say that you need it. In other words, you can lend out your "spaces" more comfortably if you make clear arrangements about their use and their return. Naturally, you will also want to show the same respect for the possessions and spaces of your siblings, being careful not to abuse the privilege of using what is theirs. This respectful "give and take" of property and space makes for respectful, loving relationships.

11. REFUSE TO FIGHT

Wrong Way:

> *David (banging loudly on door and shouting):* "GET OUT OF THE BATHROOM ALREADY — CAN'T ANYONE ELSE GET IN THERE!?"
>
> *Esther (opening door and shouting):* "YOU MUST HAVE BEEN ABSENT THE DAY THEY HANDED OUT GOOD MANNERS!"
>
> *David:* "LOOK WHO'S TALKING!"

Right Way:

> *David (banging loudly on door and shouting):* "GET OUT OF THE BATHROOM ALREADY — CAN'T ANYONE ELSE GET IN THERE!?"
>
> *Esther (opening door and speaking quietly):* "Sorry to have kept you waiting, David."

Getting involved in a fight because of a rude remark someone makes to you can cause you a lot of grief — more grief, in fact, than the rude remark itself![19] A fight doesn't happen unless two people hurt each other, physically or emotionally. If only one person says something hurtful or unpleasant then there is no fight; there is only one person being rude. However, when the other person retaliates with a rude remark of his own, then a fight has started. Often, fights escalate — that is, they get more and more hurtful with every comment that is made. That is why our Sages advise us to avoid a quarrel by simply not responding to someone's rudeness.

The person who is rude is provoking a fight. It's almost like he's sending you an invitation to a quarrel. Would you like to go along? If you want to have a quarrel, then by all means, answer back in an insulting manner. If, on the other hand, you would prefer not to have an argument, then don't answer back.

Admittedly, it takes strength of character not to insult back when someone has insulted you. Particularly if you are already in the habit of having a quick answer for siblings (or other people) who provoke you, it can be tricky to try to hold yourself back at first. However, with practice and determination, you can actually train yourself not to respond with your instinctive defensive retort.

In the "wrong" dialogue above, David provokes (starts up) and Esther retorts (answers back in kind). This will only cause bad feelings on both sides. Esther is determined to end these typical unpleasant interactions. She can't control David's tendency to provoke, but she can control her own response. This is what she decides to work on. When Esther practices not replying with a rude remark, she may make mistakes at first. When she notices she is making a mistake, she can stop herself midway into her sentence and just walk away! She doesn't have to be perfect right away; practice makes perfect!

In fact, you can train yourself to respond to a provocation as if it didn't happen at all. In the "right" dialogue above, for example, Esther answers her brother extremely politely, as if he hadn't exploded in a rude and impatient manner to her. By doing this, Esther remains in a calm, unruffled state — she doesn't upset herself at all. Moreover, she deprives her brother of the "thrill" of annoying her, probably discouraging him somewhat from trying to annoy her in the future.

Thus, when a sibling provokes you, you have a choice. You can respond in a similar, nasty way or you can respond in a mature, pleasant way. The person who is provoking is doing something quite wrong; you don't have to join him! Keep your life simple and peaceful by refusing to fight!

12. TREAT SIBLINGS THE WAY YOU WANT TO BE TREATED

Wrong Way:

> Benny: "Can I borrow your stapler, Daniel?"
>
> Daniel: "No way! You never let me use yours when I ask!"

Right Way:

> Benny: "Can I borrow your stapler, Daniel?"
>
> Daniel: "Okay. But please put it back on my desk when you're finished with it."

Often, siblings behave unkindly just to "bug" each other. This is a way of "getting back" at a sibling who has somehow aggravated you. Of course, Jewish law does not permit us to take revenge against others, nor to bear a grudge.[20] It is written, "You shall not hate your brother in your heart."[21] This means that even if your brother or sister (or any other Jew) did something unkind to you — such as refusing to lend you an article — or wronged you in some way, you are not supposed to hold the angry thought: "Well, I'll just treat him the same way." On the contrary, we are taught that if someone refuses to lend us an item on

Monday, and he comes to us on Tuesday to ask if he can borrow something from us, we are supposed to lend it to him happily.[22]

Admittedly, this takes a lot of personal development. The natural thing is to be angry at people who treat us unkindly. The natural thing is to want to treat them unkindly in return. But think: where does this cycle eventually lead? If Benny is nasty to Daniel, Daniel could choose to be nasty in return. Then Benny can feel entitled to be even more nasty to Daniel. Then Daniel can feel entitled to be even worse to Benny — and so on until it is well established that Benny and Daniel completely dislike each other and desire only to hurt each other. Clearly, neither of them profits from the "get back at him" policy.

On the other hand, if Benny is nasty to Daniel but Daniel treats Benny kindly, then Benny may be inclined to start treating Daniel somewhat better (especially if Daniel really perseveres in this kind treatment over a period of time). This better treatment makes Daniel feel good and encourages him to continue his kind treatment of Benny. The kinder he treats Benny, the kinder Benny begins to treat Daniel. Eventually, the two are good buddies who can count on each other to help out, share, and care whenever called upon. This is a real bonus for both of them.

Daniel's decision to act nicely to Benny despite Benny's unpleasant behavior ends up bringing extra happiness into his life (and his brother's, too). Sure, a decision like this requires a great deal of patience and determination. It also takes a fair amount of self-esteem: if Daniel didn't like himself, he wouldn't have been able to be nice to someone who wasn't nice to him, because he would have felt too threatened.

However, people who like themselves understand that the bad treatment they receive from another person only indicates that that person has some sort of problem.

For example, Daniel understands that Benny doesn't want to lend him things because he is insecure. Daniel doesn't blame Benny for this; if anything, he feels sorry for him. He certainly doesn't take his unkind behavior personally. By judging his brother favorably, assuming there is some good reason why his brother is not being more thoughtful toward him, Daniel is able to maintain enough good feelings to continue to act nicely toward him. If you strengthen yourself so that you are sure you are a good person, you, too, will be able to develop this patient and caring attitude — you will not need to "get back" at siblings who seem to be mean.

By following these strategies with your siblings, you are sure to have successful relationships at home. Moreover, these techniques are applicable to all of your relationships with people (e.g., friends, other relatives, and even acquaintances) and can be used to ensure your success in getting along in any situation. Try them out and see how they work for you. And remember: if at first you don't succeed, try, try again! Learning new skills always takes time and involves mistakes. Be patient, persevere, and you will definitely succeed!

4
Understanding Friends

FRIENDS ARE IMPORTANT.[1] They make life more interesting, fun, and meaningful. "A friend is there to help when one stumbles...to be a precious confidant, a source of counsel."[2] There are several different kinds of friendships, each with it's own unique characteristics.

To begin with, there are friends that are called "acquaintances." These are people that you know only slightly. You may know the name of an acquaintance, his/her age, and maybe even his/her address. You may feel friendly toward an acquaintance; you may smile whenever you meet on the street or exchange greetings. You usually do not know how an acquaintance thinks or feels about too many topics, and you don't usually know very much about what is happening in his/her life. You seldom spend leisure time with acquaintances. Most people have lots of acquaintances, including fellow students or workers, neighbors, storekeepers, and people that go to the same shul, library, and other regularly attended places.

Next, there are people who are called "companions," or more commonly, "friends." Again, a person may have many companions. These are people whom you choose to spend time with. You normally know more about companions than you know about acquaintances. The better friends you are (that is, the closer you feel to each other), the more you will know. For example, you will know something about "casual friends," including a bit about their families, some of the things they like and dislike, some of the things they can and can't do well, some of the ways they think and tend to act. Casual friends may be true friends whom you like, or they may be "friends of convenience." Friends of convenience are people whom you spend time with (maybe even a great deal of time), but whose greatest common link with you is proximity. That is, they live near you or they are in your classes or they are in some other way "convenient." Other than the convenience, you may not actually have much in common with these sorts of friends and may not have a very deep friendship with them.

You will know much more about "good friends" and have a much closer feeling toward them. You will know more about their daily routine, more about their thoughts and feelings, their typical behavior, their problems, and so on. You will have more in common with them as well — intellectually and spiritually. "We can have many companions, but only few [good] friends."[3]

All of these kinds of friends — casual, convenient, and good — can be enjoyed. You may do things with friends, go places with them, talk to them, and have fun with them. You may confide in them, ask them to listen and help you with problems. Friends share ideas and feelings. They sharpen each other's minds.[4] They celebrate events with each other. Friends help each other and support each other in lots of ways. Most people have at least one friend; some people have several friends or more.

Then there are "best friends." These are special people whom you feel very close to. "Someone who has succeeded in finding the lifelong treasure of a really true friend may be called fortunate indeed."[5] You know a lot about your best friend (including how he/she thinks and feels about most things), and your best friend knows all about you. You can share your deepest feelings with a best friend. Usually you try to spend a lot of time together or you try to speak to each other often. You know what's going on in your best friend's life. You like your best friend more than any other friend. Best friends trust each other and they can depend on each other. Some people do not have a best friend. Some people have one best friend for a while and then they change best friends. Some people have one best friend for their whole life. A few people have two best friends at a time, but this is hard to manage because best friends take a lot of time, energy, and devotion.

Some people enjoy having lots of acquaintances and friends. They like being around people and interacting with them. Others prefer to spend time at home with their families. They don't enjoy being with others so much. They may like having one or two friends or they may not want even that.

Both ways are fine. As long as a person knows how to get along with people, care for them, share with them, laugh with them, enjoy life with them, and love them, it doesn't matter whether he does this with one person or with twenty, or whether those people are family members or others. Having more friends does not prove anything. It does not make someone a better person. It only means that a person likes to spend his time with other people.

There are several reasons why people may choose not to have lots of friends. One reason is that a person may prefer to spend his time on activities like learning, reading, exercising, doing crafts, or other activities, and he may like to do these things on his own. Then there are those folks who don't seek friends because they have enough people in their own family to enjoy spending time with, and they don't need friends for companionship.

Then, too, there are people who don't have as many friends as they would like, but they really don't know how to go about getting more. So they don't even try. (These people can increase the number of their friendships by learning and practicing the friendship skills which we'll present in this chapter.)

Whether the people you choose to interact with are friends or relatives, the skills involved in building good relationships are the same. All human relationships take work. They must be nurtured and maintained just like a garden! And they yield fruits as sweet as any that we eat — for good relationships are as important to us as food itself.[6] Relationships make our lives meaningful and enjoyable. Let's see what makes them work.

BEING A FRIEND

Ruth was new in town. She was a shy sort of person who didn't make friends easily. At her new school, she went to classes but didn't talk much to people. The first day she came, a few girls welcomed her and offered to show her around. By the end of the week, however, nobody paid much attention to her. So Ruth walked through the school corridors, eyes downward, body slightly bent, keeping to herself. Her face was generally deadpan — "You can't be very expressive if nobody is talking to you," she figured. In class, too, Ruth didn't say much. When she was forced to respond to a teacher's question, she spoke quietly as a mouse, seeming to want to disappear into a hole in the wall!

Poor Ruth! It's not easy for anyone to be a new girl in school. But it's so much harder for someone who is shy! Shy people think of themselves as not having the skills to make friends quickly and easily. They sometimes think that other people are born with friendship skills whereas they were not born that way. While it is true that some people are born with a tendency to like being around people, no one is born knowing how to make and keep friends. These are skills that are learned.

Let's look at some friendship skills.

Friendship Skill #1:
CREATE A PLEASANT FIRST IMPRESSION

People are attracted to happy-looking people. Most people are not attracted to dismal or sad-looking people. We learn from our Sages that it is a mitzvah to greet everyone with a pleasant face — it makes people feel good.[7] If you concentrate on doing this mitzvah for others, you won't be thinking so much about yourself — you won't be so self-conscious. That will help you to be relaxed enough to look genuinely happy!

Pleasant-looking people keep their mouths in a slight smile or a full smile. They do not frown!

They keep their eyes open and looking around in a sincere, pleasant manner. They don't stare at people.

They don't slouch.

They speak in a clear, normal tone of voice. They don't mumble, mutter, whisper, or murmur.

You can create a pleasant impression while being yourself — you don't have to change into someone else! The idea is to put your *best* self forward, not to hide yourself from others. Be the self that you are when you're most relaxed and happy with someone. That's your natural, most attractive self; that's the one you want to present to the world.

Friendship Skill #2:
REALIZE YOU HAVE SOMETHING TO OFFER

Little kids will sometimes make friends by bringing a bag of cookies to the playground and offering one to everybody. A child who does this has "something to offer" other people. Older people don't usually hand out treats in order to make buddies, but those who have something to offer will surely make friends sooner.[8] What can you offer other people? Let's hear what some young people say they like in their friends.

Naomi:

I enjoy shopping with Miriam. She knows how to get a bargain and she knows how to find just the right item. Whenever I need to get something for myself, I call Miriam to come with me. I value her expertise.

Adam:
I really get along well with Roni. He's a top-notch student and he's willing to take the time to help me out with my schoolwork. We learn together several times a week.

Esther:
Tova has a fantastic sense of humor. I love being around her. She always cheers me up. She's so funny!

Orah:
I like spending time with Rachel because she's so undemanding. She's relaxed — no pressure, no competition. She's easy to be with. We don't have to do anything in particular in order to have fun.

David:
Dov is my best friend. He and I spend every spare moment on chess. He's a real expert. It's a pleasure to play with him.

Rena:
Sarah is a great listener. I can talk to her about any problem I have and she helps me to work it out. She's never judgmental or critical. She just helps me to think things through. That's why I like her so much.

You will be interesting to people because you have something special to offer. It could be your easygoing nature, your area of special talent or interest, your fun-loving character, your niceness, thoughtfulness, trustworthiness, or whatever. Think about yourself for a moment. What do *you* have to offer others? Write down a few things in the space on the following page.

If you wrote down lots of things, you are well on your way to making friends. If you couldn't think of too many things, think some more. Most people have lots of positive traits. Write down anything good about yourself.

Look at your list now. What you'll want to do is find people who will appreciate what you have to offer. Often, these people will be a lot like yourself. Keep your eyes open to meet people like you. But they don't have to be like you in everything. If you have something to offer — let's say a good sense of humor — then anybody who likes humor will be able to enjoy this part of you. You can be friendly with people without being really good friends with them. Being friendly means sharing what you have to offer with whoever appreciates that particular part of you.

Friendship Skill #3:
BE A GOOD LISTENER

Although it's definitely important to have something to say, it can be even more important to know how to listen to others! If you can learn to be a good listener — one who seems to hear and understand what others say — you will be well liked and appreciated by almost everyone you meet.[9]

What does it take to be a good listener? The first step is to try to really hear what the speaker is saying. Instead of thinking about what you want to say next, go slowly and really look at the person who is speaking (if you're not speaking on the telephone!). What does his/her body language tell you? How is he/she standing? What kind of facial expression is he/she wearing? What does the tone of voice tell you? How quickly or slowly, loudly or softly is he/she speaking? All of these things, *plus* the actual words of the speaker, can help you to understand what the speaker is really trying to tell you.

For example, you meet Leah walking down the street and you greet her.

You: "Hi Leah! How are you?"

Leah (pale face, eyes down, body slumped, mumbling slowly): "Oh. Hi. Fine, thanks."

From the way Leah looks and sounds, you can tell that something is wrong. She's not feeling fine at all. You have really listened by looking carefully and paying attention to every part of her communication. Words alone do not give the whole message.

Listening in this way helps you really understand a person. People need to feel understood,[10] and they appreciate those who can do this for them. Of course, you have to let the speaker know that you heard what they're telling you. This step is called "feedback." Feedback does not contain any of *your* ideas, thoughts, or feelings. It is a statement of the *speaker's* ideas, thoughts, or feelings. Sometimes it takes the form of repeating the speaker's words almost exactly (e.g., Speaker: "I hate math." Listener: "You hate math?"). Sometimes it takes the form of repeating the speaker's ideas in different words (e.g., Speaker: "I hate math." Listener: "You don't enjoy arithmetic, eh?"). Sometimes it takes the form of summing up the speaker's main idea (e.g., Speaker: "I hate math." Listener: "You and numbers don't mix"). Sometimes it takes the form of acknowledging receipt of the speaker's message (e.g., Speaker: "I hate math." Listener: "You do?" or "Hmm," or "Really?"). Sometimes it involves reading between the lines to guess what the speaker really means (e.g. Speaker: "I hate math." Listener: "You find it hard?").

Let's suppose your friend Esther makes this statement:

Esther: "I want to change schools."

You: "You want to go to a different school?"

You have given Esther feedback. You show her that you understand what she said. You did not share any of your own ideas or thoughts on the subject. You didn't offer advice. You didn't give criticism or suggestions. You didn't even show sympathy, agreement, support, or any other indication of your own attitude. In fact, Esther has no idea of how *you* feel about her idea of changing schools (providing your face and tone of voice don't give it away!). For instance, the following remarks are *not* feedback:

"What? Are you crazy? Why would you want to do that?"

"Oh, there you go again. Always wanting something new and exciting to do."

"Have you discussed this with your parents?"

"I don't. I like this school just fine."

"Wow! What a great idea!"

"So do I. I wish my parents would let me."

"Don't tell anyone!"

Since Esther just made a simple statement to you, it's not clear that she wants your advice. She certainly doesn't want your criticism. She may want to talk about her feelings but she probably doesn't want you to work it all out for her. Most people just want a chance to think things through — and a good listener helps them with that process.

Here are two examples of how the conversation could go: one with poor listening skills and the other with good listening skills (the use of feedback).

Poor Listening:

> *Esther:* "I want to change schools."
>
> *Naomi:* "Whatever for?"
>
> *Esther:* "The girls here are so snobbish. I think I'd get along better at Ohr Torah High."
>
> *Naomi:* "That's ridiculous. The girls there aren't your speed at all. You must just be in a bad mood right now."
>
> *Esther:* "No, I'm serious. Everyone here has their little clique. Apart from you, I have no friends."
>
> *Naomi:* "You have lots of friends! What about Ruth, Rachel, Miriam, Sara Leah, and Faigy?"

Esther: "Those girls aren't real friends. Sure, they sit with me at lunchtime, but we never talk on the phone or visit on Shabbos or do anything together. I want real friends."

Naomi: "Well, I think you're barking up the wrong tree. You should just try to get closer to the girls you like here. The grass is always greener on the other side, you know, but if you switch schools I bet you'll find you have no friends there either."

Good Listening:

Esther: "I want to change schools."

Naomi: "You want to change schools?"

Esther: "Yeah. The girls here are such snobs."

Naomi: "They aren't friendly toward you."

Esther: "You can say that again. I think there's a much nicer crowd at Ohr Torah High."

Naomi: "So you think you'll fit in better there."

Esther: "Definitely."

Naomi: "Hmm."

Esther: "Do you agree?"

Naomi: "Well, do you really want my opinion or do you just want me to agree?"

Esther: "No, I really want your opinion."

Naomi: "Well, I agree it's hard to get close to the girls here, but are you sure you've really tried?"

Understanding Friends

Esther: "What do you mean?"

Naomi: "Have you invited anyone to your house or called them on the phone or things like that?"

Esther: "Not really. I've been too scared to."

Naomi: "You're afraid they'll reject you?"

Esther: "I guess so. They always seem so sure of themselves and so busy."

Naomi: "They look like they know what they're doing and they haven't got time for you."

Esther: "Yeah. I guess that's silly though. I mean some of them must be human. I bet there's even a couple of really nice girls here. You know, maybe I haven't given them a proper chance."

Naomi: "Maybe you haven't."

Esther: "Thanks for listening Naomi. You've really helped me."

Naomi: "No problem!"

In the "poor listening" dialogue, Esther will likely feel that her friend Naomi just doesn't understand her. The conversation is almost like a battle, with Esther fighting to make her point and Naomi contradicting and correcting her.

In the "good listening" dialogue, Esther has a chance to talk out her problem, while Naomi gives her plenty of feedback without offering her opinion *until it's asked for.* At that point, Naomi stops giving feedback for a bit, while she offers her own ideas. Then she continues giving more feedback. Esther feels really understood. Moreover, she's able to solve her own problem and feel good about it. All she needed was the opportunity to sort out her thoughts by expressing them out loud. Naomi provided her with that opportunity by being a good listener. Her good listening skills make her a valuable friend.

Good listening in the form of feedback does not have to be used all the way through every conversation. If a friend has a problem she wants to discuss with you — that's the time to use as much feedback as you can. However, you can use bits of feedback in regular conversations, too. In addition, starting off almost any conversation with feedback is called using a "door opener." If a friend says, "Oh no! I have so much homework tonight I'll never get it finished," you can use your door opener feedback: "Boy, that sounds overwhelming." The door opener lets the speaker continue if they want to. If they don't feel a need to say any more, they won't.

On the other hand, "door closers" prevent conversations from going anywhere. They stop the speaker in his tracks so that he doesn't continue to tell you his thoughts and feelings. For example, responding, "So do I," to that speaker's remarks will probably put an end to his side of the conversation.

Try feedback listening skills on friends, parents, siblings, and other people with whom you come in contact. It's fun to see how well the technique works. Moreover, it's one of the most valuable skills to have for developing close, successful relationships.

Friendship Skill #4:
BE ASSERTIVE

Assertiveness is an important personal quality to have if you want to form true friendships. Assertiveness is the skill of being truly yourself with other people. It involves many skills: standing up for what you believe in, learning to take care of yourself, treating others respectfully, learning to ask for what you want, avoiding what you don't want, and negotiating fairly with others.

Assertive people accomplish all of this without insulting or hurting anyone. Besides being wrong,[11] causing pain to others is not the "style" of assertive people. Rather, assertive people always consider the feelings of others, treating them the way they themselves would like to be treated.[12] They are able to be sincere without being offensive.[13] They are able to look after their own needs without trampling over the needs of others, without causing disputes.[14] They don't allow themselves to be manipulated by others, for they accept responsibility for themselves.[15] They are direct.

For example, we could call Goldie an assertive young lady.

> Rachel saw Goldie sitting on a bench eating her lunch by herself. "Goldie," she called out. "How about skipping science class and going for a little shopping trip with me?"
>
> Goldie looked up. "No thanks, Rachel."
>
> "Why not Goldie? You aren't 'chicken' are you?"
>
> Goldie looked Rachel straight in the eyes. "I just don't skip classes. I don't want to. I don't like missing work and I don't like getting poor grades. You know I love shopping, though. I'd be glad to go with you after school."

Goldie was honest with her friend. She wasn't afraid to say how she really felt. She knew she had nothing to lose: people respect people who are sure of themselves. Moreover, everybody is exposed to plenty of "peer pressure" — the pressure to do what "everyone" is doing. Yet, the person who remains true to himself in every set of circumstances is the person who is truly respected. The comfortably assertive person knows how to say "no" when "yes" doesn't reflect his true personality. When speaking, Goldie used "assertive posture" — she made eye contact, she sat up straight and relaxed, she used a firm, pleasant tone of voice, and she kept her face friendly looking.

However, if Goldie hadn't been assertive, she probably would have agreed to skip the class just so that her friend wouldn't think she was "chicken." She might have ended up doing something that she didn't really want to do. This would have been *passive* behavior. Passive people allow others to make their decisions for them. They are followers who let themselves get pulled along by the crowd or by stronger personalities.

Mordy is a passive type:

> Michael saw Mordy enter the park. "Ah," he thought to himself, "just the guy I need." Michael called out: "Mordy! I need to use your bike! Quick! Bring it here, will ya?"
>
> Mordy froze. The ten-speed bike was brand new — a really expensive gift from his parents. They made him promise to take excellent care of it. And here was Michael, notorious for his careless behavior toward everything (if you happened to lend him a book, you'd never recognize it upon its return!). And he was asking for his bike! But Mordy didn't know how to say "no."

So, stammering and blushing, he answered, "Sure, Michael."

Mordy watched with a sick feeling in his stomach as Michael zoomed down the street on the shiny ten-speed. He didn't even know how long Michael would be gone. "Why did I lend it to him?" Mordy wondered to himself. "He's not even a good friend of mine. Why can't I just say no for once?"

Passive people like Mordy let others "walk all over them." They imagine that people will like them better for being so agreeable; little do they realize that the exact opposite is true! Nobody likes "doormats" who don't respect themselves. Being agreeable is a pleasant and desirable trait, but only when it is sincere. The person who acts agreeably while harboring resentment or anger — who acts agreeably only because he hasn't figured out how to be disagreeable in an appropriate, pleasant way — is being both dishonest and destructive in his relationships. Passivity thus prevents a person from enjoying sincere friendships.

Passive people withdraw from others out of fear of being themselves. They sort of disappear into the woodwork as if they have something to hide. They don't say what they want, don't lead the way, and don't express their own opinions. Their body language also helps them disappear. Often, they speak so quietly you have to strain to hear them. They don't look people in the eye. They slump over and/or lean against walls. Their eyes look pleading or sad. The whole message is, "I'm not really here. Whatever *you* want is okay with me. I have no thoughts or ideas. I'm not interesting or important."

Passive people end up hurting themselves by denying their own, valid needs. They don't give themselves a chance to get what they want out of life; they don't allow themselves to reach their own potential. People aren't born passive. They learn to be that way — and they can learn to be assertive instead.

A third personality style is called *aggressive*. Aggressive people get what they want by intimidating others. They like to run the show, make the decisions, and lead the way. However, they don't mind if they hurt other people in the process. Aggressive people can be insulting, sarcastic, or rude. They interrupt others, discount their thoughts and feelings, and generally "walk all over" them.

Esti is your typical aggressive person:

> Risa rang Esti's doorbell. Soon enough, Esti answered.
> "Hi. I'm ready. Let's go shopping."
> Risa paused.
> "What's the matter?" asked Esti.
> "Well," started Risa, "are you sure you want to wear that skirt? I mean, it barely covers your knees."
> "OF COURSE I WANT TO WEAR IT! WHAT ARE YOU — MY MOTHER OR SOMETHING? 'SHORT' IS IN THE EYES OF THE BEHOLDER — I THINK YOU WEAR YOURS RIDICULOUSLY LONG, ACTUALLY."
> Risa was taken aback. Esti was obviously angry at her remark, although Risa thought she was being helpful. "Look, I didn't mean to insult you," Risa said. "I thought maybe you didn't realize how short that skirt was. I didn't want you to be embarrassed or anything."
> Esti huffed and bellowed: "WELL, LET'S STOP TALKING ABOUT IT ALREADY. ARE YOU COMING OR NOT?"

Esti's aggressive response is characteristically loud and harsh. It is accompanied by typically aggressive body posture: lots of hand movements, glaring eyes, mad face, tense body. Risa feels uncomfortable in the face of this aggressive attack. She feels put down. Esti is someone she'll try hard to avoid from now on. Aggressive people tend to lose friends because of the way they treat them.

Esti didn't have to be aggressive. If she really believed her skirt length was halachically permissible, she could have said so in a pleasant, assertive way. For example, she might have responded, "I appreciate your concern, Risa, but I always wear my skirts this length. My folks have no objection, and it fits the standards of my school, so I assume it's okay." In an *assertive* mode, Esti could take into consideration the feelings of her friend and respond sensitively to her. In an *aggressive* mode, Esti wouldn't care how her friend felt. She'd be more interested in making her point, in getting her way, in doing what *she* wanted. Like passive behavior, aggressive behavior is learned. It can be unlearned and replaced with assertive behavior, which is more conducive to having healthy friendships.

Then there's the "passive-aggressive" type of person. This kind of person lacks the courage to say what he really feels or to act the way he really wants to act, so he gets his message across in a sort of underhanded way, even while seeming to passively accept someone's else's directive. For example, Leah responds in a passive-aggressive mode in the following situation:

> Leah's best friend Sarah has been acting a bit cool lately. She hasn't returned Leah's telephone calls. She hasn't made arrangements to get together on the week-

end. She's made herself generally unavailable. Leah is upset. However, instead of confronting Sarah directly, she has chosen to demonstrate her feelings through her behavior.

"I'll show her," Leah thinks to herself. "Just wait until she wants to be with me. I think I'll be 'busy' just like she seems to be these days."

Just then, Sarah passes by. "Leah, do you want to meet me at the library tonight to do that research for the history assignment?"

"Sure," Leah replies. "I'll be there around eight."

Eight o'clock finds Sarah sitting in their usual study spot alone. Eight-thirty passes, then nine, then nine-thirty. Realizing that Leah isn't likely to show up, Sarah finishes her work and goes home.

The next morning, she sees Leah on her way to class. "Hey, Leah! What happened last night? Where were you?" she calls out.

Leah looks blank, then responds innocently, "Last night? Oh, I'm sorry Sarah. I completely forgot. I got tied up with some things. Sorry about that."

Leah is showing her displeasure in a passive-aggressive style. Her anger is expressed in "innocently" disappointing her friend. People who use this style tend to "forget" things, or arrive "late," or "accidentally" break, damage, or lose things. Their words say, "It's okay," but their actions say, "I'm mad!"

Assertive people are able to say "no" with their words. They are not afraid of disapproval because they know that they are entitled to refuse certain requests — even without providing reasons. For example, a young woman who has a very small wardrobe may comfortably say, "No, I'm sorry, but I don't lend my clothes out." She needn't passively lend them out, fearing to be ridiculed. She needn't sarcastically refuse, implying that the borrower was making a ridiculous request. She needn't explain that she can't afford to clean or replace items and therefore doesn't lend them. She knows, after all, that she does many acts of kindness for others, including lending certain things. However, she just cannot lend her clothes due to her situation. She is allowed to say no. Moreover, assertive people know how to refuse in a polite, caring way (e.g., "If you need to borrow a dress, maybe I could help you find one").

Assertive people also know how to tell a friend that they are disappointed, hurt, or upset. ("You know, I really take good care of my books, and I'm really upset at the way you returned this one. The front cover was ripped and there was food on a few pages.") Instead of acting hurtful in return, they know how to ask for what they need. For example, they can say things like: "You seem to be distant lately. Is there anything wrong? Did I upset you or something?" If people act in an unfair way toward an assertive person, the assertive person is not intimidated. For example, if someone says, "Why do you ask what's wrong? You must be imagining things. Maybe you're paranoid," the assertive person would maintain her calm and confidence, responding with something like, "No. I'm sure you haven't telephoned as often as you usually do and you haven't spent the usual amount of time with me at school. I don't mind — I only wanted to clear the air if your behavior is on account of something I did to upset you. If you're telling me that you're not upset, then great. That's all I wanted to know!"

Assertive people aren't afraid to ask for anything they

need: information ("Can you tell me how to get to Center Street?"), affection ("Mom, I need a hug"), assistance ("I can't figure out how to do this math problem — can you explain it to me?"), companionship ("Can you come over to my place on Sunday?"), peace and quiet ("Could you please speak more quietly so I can concentrate on my work?"), or freedom from harassment ("Please don't call me names"). Asking for something does not cheapen the product. For example, it is nice if someone gives you a spontaneous hug, but the hug is equally valuable and enjoyable if it is given after you asked for it.

Being able to ask for what you want is a valuable skill that has the power to increase your happiness and success in life. One way to improve your "asking skills" is to close your eyes, imagine yourself in various situations in which you want something from someone, and imagine yourself asking for exactly what you want. Imagine the person giving you what you asked for, and imagine your feelings of gladness. After a few "imagining sessions" start asking for things in real life. It'll get easier every time.

As you can see, assertiveness involves lots of different skills. Knowing how to ask for something, knowing how to say no, and knowing how to be sincere and kind are all part of being assertive. You'll know you are being assertive if you can say what you think and feel while remaining polite, caring, and honest. If you find yourself being angry, bullied, intimidated, or sneaky, then you are not being assertive.

Assertive people make good friends because they are honestly themselves. They assert their own unique personalities, which makes them interesting and attractive. Practice assertive behavior as much as you can and you'll see for yourself how it affects your relationships and your happiness!

**Friendship Skill #5:
DEVELOP QUALITIES OF A GOOD FRIEND**

People usually try and find others who are like themselves to be friends with. However, once you find someone who has traits in common with you, that person won't remain a friend for long unless he has some basic "friendship qualities." These are the qualities that people say they want in their friends. They are qualities you should work on developing if *you* want to be a good friend.

To help you get a clearer picture of how you *should* behave as a friend, here are some examples of how *not* to be!

Fickle Faigy

A friend loves at all times...[16]

Fickle Faigy is your friend — and then she isn't. For some period of time she calls you on the phone, sits with you at lunchtime, visits on Shabbos, and spends every other free moment by your side. Then suddenly she doesn't call, doesn't visit, doesn't show up. She's spending time with a new friend. She can't seem to manage having two close friends at a time, so she just tends to switch her alliances without saying anything to her former best buddy. Later, she may call you again and, if you permit it, renew the former closeness. Then — she's off again. On and off, hot and cold — that's Fickle Faigy.

Always Late Leah

"A person who fulfills the commandment to love a fellow Jew will not keep people waiting."[17]

If you want to get somewhere on time, don't go with Always Late Leah. If you arrange for her to meet you at 3 p.m. — good luck! If you arrange to go with her, don't bother standing by your door waiting for her to arrive. Have a seat! Or better still, go back to bed! Always Late Leah has hundreds of excuses and apologies, but the bottom line is that she is always late. It can be very annoying.

Dishonest Deena

"Keep far from a false matter..."[18]

Dishonest Deena doesn't tell it like it is. She may lie straight out — but more likely, she's just sneaky. Even though she's your "best friend" she somehow forgets to tell you that she's going away for the weekend, until you happen to invite her over. She's not "up-front" with you; she keeps everything a secret, including her plans, her activities, and her reasons for doing things. Why all the mystery? On the other hand, if you share a secret of your own with Dishonest Deena, even though she promises never to breathe a word of it, somehow it slips out and suddenly the whole world knows! In fact, Dishonest Deena encourages her friends to share every detail of their lives with her — she can't stand secrets when they're secrets from her! Dishonest Deena may do things she knows she's not allowed to do — she breaks the rules because rules are for everyone but her. Of course she tries not to get caught. If she does get caught then she tries to lie her way out of it! Dishonest Deena thinks she's clever but she's really dumb: besides being prohibited by the Torah, dishonesty is a trait that loses lots of friends.

Really Rude Rachel

> *"And you shall not hurt the feelings of one another..."*[19]

If you're looking for an insult, then just call Really Rude Rachel. "Is that sweater from a second-hand store or did you get it new?" Really Rude Rachel may ask you in front of ten curious onlookers. "Are you handing in your assignment early again? What's the matter — do you have ants in your pants or something?" she inquires. If you happen to be standing in the path of a Really Rude Rachel, watch out — she may push and shove her way past you without so much as an "excuse me, please" and "thank you." In fact, manners are definitely not her area of expertise. Since Really Rude Rachel lacks sensitivity to the feelings of others (although she's very careful to take care of her own feelings and needs), she doesn't make a very good friend.

Sarah Status Seeker

> *"...They appear as friends when it is to their own advantage but they do not stand by a person..."*[20]

Sarah Status Seeker loves you to bits but you have to wonder — is it *you* she loves, or is it your beautiful house, your prestigious family, or your fabulous wealth? Strange how she doesn't talk to any of the nice girls who don't happen to come from such wealthy or established families as your own. Doesn't Sarah Status Seeker value people for their fine character traits? Funny how she clings to your crowd and virtually snubs everyone else. Or *is* it funny?

Rena Rebel

> *"He who goes with the wise shall become wise, while he who associates with fools shall suffer."*[21]

There are some people who should be avoided rather than befriended, and Rena Rebel is one of them. Rena Rebel doesn't fit into the regular crowd — she's definitely different. She covers up her disappointment at her academic failure by pretending school doesn't matter. She stops trying to learn so that she can blame her failure on not trying rather than on not having what it takes. But she wants to pull you down with her (it's lonely being different) so she invites you to do things which will jeopardize your own academic performance. Since Rena Rebel doesn't get along with her family, she may try to turn you against yours as well. Again, she may invite you to join in pranks which will further alienate you from your parents and siblings, such as staying out past your curfew, going where you're not permitted to go, doing what you're not allowed to do. Although Rena thinks of herself as being really "with it" she's actually really "without it" — without the good behavior and character traits which are so necessary in a friend.

Finicky Freda

> *"Do not hate one person to keep the love of another."*[22]

Finicky Freda likes you but she doesn't like anyone else. Or, she likes you and she likes her own set of friends but she doesn't like *your* other friends. In other words, if you want to get together with Finicky Freda you certainly can — but be sure not to invite anyone else! In fact, when you're with Finicky Freda don't even think of speaking to anyone else. She'll make it clear to you that those other people aren't worth your trouble. Finicky Freda brings tension into your life because she makes friendship so complicated. She has high standards — a person practically has to pass a test in order to be her friend. She thinks she's kind of special and other people (apart from you, of course) just don't measure up. So being with her makes you feel both good and bad. Best to drop her; you can find other friends with whom you'll feel just plain good — not bad at all!

Horribly Hurt Hannah

> *"One who looks for a friend without faults, will have none."*[23]

You disappointed her. You said you'd be at her place at 2:30 and you arrived at 2:40. She'll never forgive you. Horribly Hurt Hannah can't bear disappointment in human relationships. If it's not perfect, it's not good enough. Of course, it's never perfect because people just aren't perfect. Inevitably her friends let her down: one stretches the truth on one occasion; one borrows a book and neglects to return it; one forgets to return her call *twice*; one says something slightly sarcastic; one studies with someone else when she usually studies with *her*; one fails to comment on her brand new hair style. People are disappointing and Horribly Hurt Hannah just can't take it. Instead of relaxing and realizing that all people have faults and make mistakes, Horribly Hurt Hannah makes a federal case out of the failings of her friends, refusing to remain friends with such imperfect specimens. Naturally, Horribly Hurt Hannah has a rapid change-over of friends, because until she learns to be more forgiving and accepting, more flexible and comfortable with people as they are (including their faults), she can never have a friend for long.

Trying Talia

"If you want your companion to hate you, keep visiting him constantly, and if you want him to love you, visit him after long intervals."[24]

Trying Talia tries too hard. When she decides she wants to be your friend she *really* works at it, not being patient enough to let friendship develop slowly and gradually over time. She calls you three times a night and becomes a virtual shadow in the daytime, following you around everywhere. She even starts to talk like you and walk like you, using your favorite phrases and mannerisms. If she senses you're put off by something she had said or done, she apologizes profusely and repeatedly — she's just *so* sorry, really she is! She may try to win your favor again by treating you to doughnuts or other little presents — or she may just offer you such things as a way of "buying" your friendship. Of course, if you don't reciprocate all of this attention, Talia will whine and complain: "Why don't you ever call me? Why don't you ever invite me over?" Talia doesn't let you breathe. She just tries too hard to be your friend!

Miserable Miriam

"Receive every person with joy."[25]

When someone comes to you with a problem, you like to help, right? And all people have problems and deserve a sympathetic ear and a helping hand. But what about people who complain about their lives only in order to make conversation? They think that the sympathy they get for their troubles will lead to friendship. Miserable Miriam is one of those people with lots of complaints. She wants to tell you all of them all of the time. She wants you to know that she's had the flu six times this year, and she doesn't have enough money to buy what she wants, and her back hurts her today, and on and on she goes. But what Miserable Miriam doesn't realize is that she's really a bore! Although most people are willing to help when needed, people don't enjoy listening to problems non-stop; they like to be with others who cope with life and have a happy side. In fact, Miserable Miriam has a happy, coping side to her, but she's just neglecting to share it. So, if it's sympathy you want, then complain all you wish. But if it's friendship you're looking for, then ask for help only when you really need it, and be sure to show others the side of you that is bright, successful and functional — they'll appreciate it!

If you see yourself in any of these character sketches, don't be alarmed. We have all made mistakes like these at some point. The idea is to try to avoid behaving in ways that will harm our relationships. Anyone who routinely behaves like the people described above will have trouble getting along with others sooner or later.

Having friends and being involved in human relationships can cause a certain amount of aggravation and frustration. However, this is a small price to pay for the enormous satisfaction and pleasure that companionship brings. So practice these friendship skills on everyone you know — and enjoy lots of successful relationships!

5
Being Happy

WHAT IS HAPPINESS? What is the path to happiness? Even though we're supposed to be happy,[1] many people don't seem to know the answer to these two questions.

First, let's define happiness. Happiness is a feeling of pleasure and satisfaction, a positive emotion which makes one comfortable and pleased. It can be as intense as joy or as mild as contentment. Being happy can occur at any time of day and does not depend on outside activities such as "having fun" or "succeeding academically" or "being popular." In fact, happiness is an inner state, dependent only on one's thoughts.

Of course, arranging one's thoughts to bring happiness requires work; happiness does not come by itself. On the contrary, what comes by itself is negativity and unhappiness. Left to our natural inclinations, we think and behave in ways that prevent our happiness.

For example, there is a human tendency to focus on what is going wrong in life, rather than to focus on what is going right. At home, for instance, typical parents notice what their children do *incorrectly* rather than what they do correctly!

"This morning, I was listening to my mother get the younger kids ready for school. She told my brother to pick his pajamas up off the floor and brush his teeth. She told my sister to eat more quickly because the bus was coming soon. She told my other sister that she should have done her homework last night instead of at the breakfast table. She told me to stop standing in front of the mirror and help her out more! It seemed none of us could do anything right!"

Of course, all the children in this family were doing many things right. The little brother had made his bed; the sister had made her own breakfast; the other sister had got up early enough to be able to do her unfinished schoolwork, and the eldest had completely straightened up her room before coming to breakfast. However, it is the natural tendency of parents not to notice these "good" things and only notice (and comment on) the things that are going wrong.

Similarly, people of every age notice what they're displeased with and think about those things often.

"What have I got to be happy about? I'm too fat, my clothes are ugly, I have no friends, I'm doing terrible in school, and my parents pick on me all day."

A person who thinks like this is going to have an awful lot of trouble being happy! This is all the more true if the person thinks of his problems as being permanent (they'll never end) and pervasive (they completely ruin his life).

And the bad news is that things will never get much better for such a person: people who focus on the negative aspects of life today will tend to continue to focus on the negative things that tomorrow brings — and tomorrow is *guaranteed* to bring plenty of them. Life is full of problems, big ones and small ones. Every single day brings a new set of annoyances: someone who's supposed to call, doesn't; you misplace your glasses, keys, or favorite pen; your hair dryer breaks; the school play is canceled; camp turns out to be too expensive; someone insults you or criticizes you...and on and on it goes. No one is immune. Life is like that.

Therefore, in order to achieve a level of happiness, you must learn to *look at what's going right*. You must learn to appreciate all the good that is going on in your life.[2] Unhappiness is only a bad habit — the habit of focusing on what is wrong in your life, wishing that things were better. Happiness is also a habit — the habit of thinking about and enjoying all the good things that happen in each day.

Happiness Skill #1:
LOOK FOR THE GOOD

Thus, the first step is to become a detective searching for good things all day long. Was breakfast good? Enjoy! Be grateful![3] Remember that some people don't have breakfast, let alone a good one. Were you able to feed yourself that meal? Be happy! Read some biographies of people whose handicaps prevent them from achieving this skill — or better yet, take a tour of an institution for the physically handicapped. You'll never take this ability for granted again!

Did you leave the house dressed comfortably against

the wind? Feel blessed! Read some stories of people whose poverty was so intense that they couldn't afford a sweater or coat — this will add to your gratitude each time you dress.

Did someone wish you a pleasant day as you left your home? Think of those who have no one to send them off with love!

There are so many things to be happy about before you've even left the house in the morning — things you normally don't think about because you're too busy concentrating on the things that bother you! What seem like small pleasures are things that — were you to lose them, Heaven forbid — you'd sorely miss. And many times, that's what it takes to make a person realize that he *should* have been happy. When someone loses one of life's taken-for-granted, overlooked gifts, he finally recognizes the pleasure that was there to be enjoyed — too late.

Don't let this happen to you! As you go through every hour of your day, think about the things that are good in that hour. Maybe even take the time to write them down so that you can read the list over whenever you want to increase your happiness. If you talked on the phone to a friend, you can write down that you have a friend. Or you can write down that it was nice to talk on the phone to someone. If someone gave you a compliment or praise, you can write down that someone was kind to you. If you found the weather pleasant, you can write that down. If you earned some spending money, you can write that down. Anything and everything that feels good to you should be included on your list.

Also, put the things that make you feel happy *up front*

in your life: put photographs on your wall that make you remember happy times; put signs on your wall that remind you to be grateful; keep a journal of positive happenings; talk about good things to your friends and family.

"I try not to talk about unhappy things like mean people, unfair situations, worrisome events, and so on. Of course, if I'm trying to solve a particular problem, I'll talk to a friend about that just to get some help in solving it. But I never complain about things just for the fun of complaining, because I don't find it's fun! In fact, I find that I feel less happy the more I think about or talk about unpleasant things."

Keep your mind off what you feel you are lacking. Don't think (and don't talk) about all the things that are missing or "wrong" with your life. That only brings you unhappiness.

Remember that all people tend to think that happiness will come to them when "such and such" happens. "Such and such" could be any event that a person feels he needs to complete his life: when she becomes skinny, or when he gets rich, or when her mother loves her, or when he succeeds in school, or when she has a best friend, or when he has hundreds of friends, or when her hair looks normal, or when his complexion clears up, or when she gets married, or when she has children, or when he has his own house, and on and on go the possibilities. However, if happiness is in fact to come, it must come long before any "such and such" happens, for no one ever has all his wishes fulfilled.[4] Your happiness cannot depend on any outside factor. You need to create your happiness by enjoying what you have now.[5]

Happiness Skill #2:
WATCH YOUR LANGUAGE

The words you use to describe your feelings and responses to life actually shape and determine the level of happiness you can achieve.[6] Very negative words make you feel very unhappy. Very positive words make you feel very happy.

Everybody has both negative and positive experiences in life. In fact, as we've just mentioned, everybody has many things that go wrong every day and many things that go right as well. How do you describe what happens to you? When you misplace your book, for example, do you say to yourself, "I'M GOING CRAZY!"? Or, when you fail a test do you say, "I CAN'T STAND IT!"? Or, when your brother provokes you relentlessly do you scream, "I HATE YOU!"?

Intense negative phrases like these cause you to have intense negative feelings. However, if you make it a point to use less negative expressions when describing unpleasant events, you will find that you don't feel so unhappy! For example, try these replacement phrases:

"I prefer not doing math," instead of *"I hate doing math."*

"I feel challenged by having to give a speech," instead of *"I'm petrified to have to give a speech."*

"I'm a little down right now," instead of *"I'm depressed."*

"I'm a bit nervous to be doing this for the first time," instead of *"I'm terrified to be doing this for the first time."*

"I'm annoyed," instead of *"I'm furious."*

Notice that words like "prefer not," "feel challenged," and "annoyed" are not as emotionally loaded as words like "hate," "petrified," and "furious." Less intense negative words lead to less intense negative feelings. Another way to decrease negative intensity is to put a belittling adjective in front of a negative word or phrase. For example, instead of saying that you're "angry," you could say that you're "*a bit* upset." Or, instead of saying that you're "miserable" you could say that you're "*a little* down." Or, instead of saying that you're "frantic" you could say that you're "*somewhat* concerned." The belittling words — "a bit," "a little," and "somewhat" — decrease the negative intensity of a more emotionally charged word and thereby reduce the intensity of your unhappy feeling.

Similarly, if you want to increase your feelings of happiness, you can increase the intensity of your positive vocabulary. For example, if someone asks you how you are, instead of replying, "Fine, thanks," try answering something like "Great!" or even "Spectacular!" If you want to tell someone that the meal he prepared for you was very nice, instead of saying, "Everything is very good," try saying, "I just love everything you made!" or "It's scrumptious!" In describing a book you read, instead of saying it was "interesting" say it was "fascinating." Instead of saying that the weather is "nice" say that the weather is "fantastic" or "perfect" or "gorgeous." Instead of saying that the music tape you just listened to was "really good" say it was "incredible" or "phenomenal."

Notice that words like "spectacular," "scrumptious," "gorgeous," and "incredible" are much more intense than words like "nice," "good," and "fine." They're sure to make you enjoy life more because of that intensity.

Watch your choice of words: choose mild and "belittled"

words to describe negative states; choose strong, vibrant words to describe positive states. Notice how your happiness is affected by taking control of your language in this way.

**Happiness Skill #3:
PURSUE SERENITY**

Worry robs a person of happiness and destroys his life! Our Sages warn us not to indulge in this harmful habit.[7] Thinking thoughts about bad things that might happen causes you to suffer before the bad events have even taken place. In most cases, these bad events never even happen — so you've completely wasted time you could have used for being happy!

Worrying occurs when you let your mind "wander." Actually, it's not wandering at all — you are really *directing* it to conjure up scary thoughts and ideas. Thoughts don't just "pop" into your head from nowhere — you have to put them there yourself. If you don't prosper from what you've been putting there (i.e., you're not getting happier), why not change your input? Fill your mind with some *terrific* things that could happen in your future. Change your "videotapes"!

You see, worries are like scary movies that we play in our heads — that's why we might refer to them as videotapes. Here's an example:

"I have to take my driving test next week. I just know I'm going to fail! I can just picture what's going to happen: I'll be trying to park the car in a tiny, little space, and I'll never be able to line it up properly, and I'll probably even smash

into the car in front of me or something dumb like that."

Naturally, on the day of the test, this worrier will have sweaty palms and a racing heart. Her videotapes will have successfully terrorized her. As a result, her performance on the test will be impaired — fear immobilizes people and constricts their abilities.

Fortunately, you can just pull out scary videotapes and replace them with reassuring, positive ones. For example:

"I'm picturing my driving test that is scheduled for next week: I'm going to get in that car and really show them what I know. When I go to park the car, I'll line it up carefully and do a perfect parallel park. I'll be just the right distance from the cars in front of me and in back of me."

Changing to a positive videotape not only increases your feelings of happiness and pleasure in life, but also adds to your success. Psychological studies have shown that picturing successful outcomes (imagining yourself succeeding in a situation) dramatically increases your chances for actual success.

In addition, playing the "successful outcome" movie can actually help you to identify the steps that you need to take to achieve such an outcome. For example, if you picture yourself giving a successful public speech, you will notice that you stand up straight, speak loudly and clearly with good intonation, use humor and interesting stories, and so on. All of these characteristics of your successful movie are actually the necessary components for your success in reality; therefore, your video can help you to rehearse those steps that must be taken in order to do well.

Playing positive videotapes can only enhance your happiness. If the event which you are thinking about actually turns out poorly (e.g., you fail the driving test), at least you spent the previous days in a relaxed and happy state (unlike the situation in which you play scary videotapes and spend the days before the test in a state of tension and anxiety).

And even if the event does turn out poorly, there's no need to upset your basic serenity. If you tried your best, you can do no more than that. Not all events are within our control. In fact, a truly happy person does not allow his happiness to be dependent on any external factors which he can't control.[8] Rather, he accepts whatever comes his way, understanding that each challenge can help him develop in some way and each contains some benefit to him.[9] Having to take a driving test twice, for example, may force a person to learn a certain driving skill to a much higher level than he would otherwise have done, and he'll retain that skill for the rest of his life!

A serene attitude can be acquired in other ways as well. For example, if you find yourself worrying about something, you can use that as a signal to *do something constructive* about that situation. If you're worrying about a test you're going to have, use the worry as a cue to prepare yourself for that test (i.e., study!). If you're worrying about whether you'll have enough money for some necessity, use that as a cue to plan how to obtain the money you need. If you're worrying about whether something dangerous will happen, use that as a cue to set up some reasonable precautions. In other words, never permit your mind to conjure up these scary ideas for more than a second or two. Once you realize there's a problem, either change your videotape or do something constructive toward solving the problem.

In addition, it has been found that people who know how to fully relax themselves and take control of their thought processes are able to achieve the greatest sense of serenity and joy. Many people seem to be at the mercy of their overworked minds, always thinking a jumble of thoughts — thoughts that cause them anxiety and distress, thoughts without focus. Learn to control your mind and you will be able to harness your energy for pure happiness.

Here's one way of acquiring this skill:

1) Find a five-minute period when you can be alone and undisturbed.

2) Sit or lie in a comfortable, relaxed position.

3) Lightly close your eyes and slow down your breathing to a nice, slow, rhythmic pace.

4) Say one word over and over again in your mind for about three minutes. (The word should be one of the following: happy, joyful, calm, serenity, peaceful.) Gently push all other thoughts out of your mind as they arise, and return to your word.

5) Do this exercise once or twice a day. As your concentration improves, you can lengthen the period of repetition to as long as ten or fifteen minutes if you like.

This exercise gives you practice in taking control of your thought process. The expertise you gain from it will carry over into all your daily thinking. With your increased control, it will be easy for you to order your thoughts (decide what you want to think about), think in a clear fashion (solve problems, create plans, set goals, focus on your subject), and remove distracting or depressing thoughts from your mind.

All of these techniques — changing to positive videotapes, doing something constructive about a future challenge, and learning to control your thoughts — will help you to maintain the serenity so crucial to your happiness.

**Happiness Skill #4:
AVOID ANGER**

Anger robs people of happiness.[10] It is so exhausting, so draining. It leaves you feeling upset and irritable for hours. It drags you away from happiness, demanding your total attention. And it brings to the surface your basest character, your most horrid tendencies, while burying your intelligence, kindness, and goodness.

Therefore, the less you indulge in anger, the happier you will be. Each anger-free day is a pleasanter day, a day open to all sorts of possibilities and potentials. Of course, everyone would like to be free of anger. A common thought is, "I would love it if other people would stop making me so mad. After all, I don't like being angry." Yet, the truth is that other people are *not* the cause of your anger! *You* are!

What causes anger, like all other emotions, is your own thought process. That's the good news. Since you are in charge of your thinking process, you can change your thoughts to those that don't lead to anger. But you must accept this responsibility for your mood completely. You must realize that other people don't make you angry: they only create a situation which you *choose* to respond to in an angry fashion.

"My little sister went into my drawer when I wasn't home and took my glue. I was furious!"

"My little sister went into my drawer when I wasn't home and took my glue. When I found it, I told her not to do that again. But I had to hide my smile — she was so cute!"

How one responds to any "provocation" depends very much on what one thinks. For example, if you think to yourself, "How DARE my sister touch my things without permission!" then you'll put yourself into a rage. (This kind of anger comes from arrogance.)[11] On the other hand, if you think, "Little kids get into mischief; I was the same when I was that age," then you'll be tolerant and patient and maybe even mildly amused by the same "provocation."

But how can you arrange your thoughts so that you'll be anger-free? Here are some strategies:

1) Don't think in terms of your "rights" (how people should be treating you) — always think in terms of how you can help others (especially your family members).[12] Thinking of your "rights" leads to anger because other people will inevitably trample over them. If you think more about what you can do for people than what they should do for you, you'll be happier because you put yourself in the driver's seat: *you* control what you do for others. On the other hand, you are at the mercy of others when you wait for them to fulfill your "rights" — and you may have a long wait, too!

2) When others insult you, remember that *they* are doing something wrong[13] — they obviously have some kind of problem. Rather than anger, feel pity for them (that they don't know how to control themselves better or communicate in a more healthful manner).

3) When others criticize you, remember that you have no reason to defend yourself: either they are wrong in their criticism (in which case, you can gently correct their impression), or they are right (in which case, you can gratefully work on improving some aspect of yourself, a bonus for you).[14] Defending yourself only leads to arguments and increased anger.

4) If you make it a rule to speak in a pleasant tone of voice to all people at all times (no matter what!) you will not get angry.[15]

5) Keep in mind that your happiness is important: why let someone's behavior (usually involving a fairly minor or trivial incident) take away your happiness even for a few minutes? (And, unfortunately, once you allow yourself to get angry, that emotion tends to linger, physically and emotionally, well beyond "a few minutes.")

6) If you make it your habit to judge people favorably,[16] you will always be looking for a good reason why someone might have done whatever it is he did. Even if the only reason you can come up with is that the person is human and made a mistake, it'll be sufficient. After all, aren't *you* allowed to make mistakes also? By judging people positively, you'll become quick to forgive them and you won't get angry.

7) If you know that someone will do something that will upset you, picture the whole scene *before* it happens; that way, you'll be calmer when it actually takes place. Also, you can picture yourself responding in a really good way — a way that helps the situation. Then, when the scenario takes place, you'll know just what to do.[17]

8) When dealing with someone who angered you (espe-

cially a family member), pretend that there is someone important in the room with you, someone you'd like to impress. This will help you to handle yourself well and be calmer.

9) Get enough sleep each night. As sleep decreases, irritability increases.

If you do get angry once in a while, you can pull yourself out of it quickly by refusing to think about the event that upset you. Have a "let's get on with life" attitude; don't dwell on what went wrong — think about how to make the future better.

If someone did something wrong to you, increase your happiness in life by forgiving him! The more you hold on to your anger and resentment, the more *you* suffer. Sometimes people think that their anger will prevent the other person from hurting them again. Anger spoils human relationships; it doesn't heal them. The best way to improve a relationship and/or prevent a person from hurting you is to forgive him and "make up." Even if the other person doesn't want to get along with you, your anger is unnecessary and even self-destructive. Do yourself a favor and forgive him anyway — you'll have greater serenity in your life.

If it's your parents that you're angry at, and you can't, for some reason, work it out with them, try to get help from a trusted neighbor, teacher, rabbi, or counselor. Don't allow yourself to carry a burden of anger that will destroy your happiness.

Reducing anger in your life will increase your happiness immensely. Do it and see!

Happiness Skill #5:
MANAGE YOUR MOODS

Young people, among others, are prone to "moods." Sometimes they are ecstatically happy and other times morosely depressed. Sometimes they are perfectly calm and other times they are unpleasantly irritable. Of course, people of all ages have their "moods," but young people seem to have more than their fair share!

Naturally, it's not the "up" moods that are distressing. Rather, it is the negative moods — the depressed feelings and the cranky ones — that cause the problems. A person who finds fault with too many things each day simply cannot enjoy life. Being in a "black" mood causes you to look at everything from a black perspective: you find the younger children in the family excruciatingly annoying; you can't stand your teachers; your classmates seem immature and superficial; your parents are impossibly demanding. Everything seems wrong. (And the good things are all overlooked and taken for granted.)

"When I'm in a 'mood' nobody can do anything right. I don't like anyone and I don't like anything. I don't like the food that's available. I don't like any of the things I have to do that day (even things that are supposed to be 'fun,' like swimming or whatever). I don't like any of the clothes in my cupboard. Nothing pleases me at all. In fact, if people try to cheer me up, I turn down their offers and their advice without so much as a 'thank you but no thanks.' Off and on I just feel like screaming and going hysterical (acting like a two-year-old having a tantrum)! Sometimes I'm in a bad mood for a few minutes; other times it can last a few hours;

Being Happy

once it lasted a couple of days. I'm pretty sure nobody enjoys my company at those times, but I don't care while it's happening. I don't care about anything."

Obviously, such moods interfere with one's happiness. Are moods unavoidable? Are they just a part of life? Yes and no. Yes, all people will experience mood swings occasionally, so we could say that they are just part of life. But, no, they are not completely unavoidable. In fact, if you follow a few simple precautions, you should be able to reduce your bad moods to very near zero. Here's how:

1) Get enough sleep. Young people can easily need eight to ten hours a night. Being short on sleep causes almost everyone to be in an irritable mood the next day.

2) Eat real food. Real food consists of meat, fish, dairy products, fruits, vegetables, and bread products. Non-real food consists of sugary/fatty snacks such as potato chips, soft drinks, chocolate bars, sweet buns and pastries, coffee, and tea. Real food nourishes you; non-real food depletes you and, by upsetting your chemical balance, sends you into bad moods.

3) Be sociable — call your friends. Isolation (sitting at home alone) can bring on or intensify bad moods. Being with people you enjoy keeps your mood positive.

4) Keep busy. Throw yourself into activities; never allow yourself to sit around being bored (that's a sure invitation for a bad mood). Study, read, do exercise, do arts and crafts, clean up and organize something, help someone, practice or learn a new skill, write a letter or a book, bake, sew, or build something — just pick something and do it! Busy people don't have the time to indulge in mood-

iness — nor the inclination.

Following these four rules can reduce your moods significantly and increase your happiness proportionately!

**Happiness Skill #6:
BE A PROBLEM-SOLVER**

Everybody has problems. A problem is actually nothing more than a challenge — a situation which is uncomfortable and requires your attention in order to reduce that discomfort. Problems needn't interfere with your happiness (otherwise nobody could ever be happy!). However, problems can prevent happiness in those people who don't know how to manage them.

"I have lots of problems in my life. My parents argue a lot — that's one problem. I have to share my room with two sisters I don't get along with — that's another problem. I'm having a lot of trouble with my grades in school — that's a third one. My best friend recently became best friends with my worst enemy — that's yet another. Since I have so many problems, there's no way I can be happy. In fact, all I think about all day is one problem or another. I'm constantly depressed."

How can one successfully manage so many problems? Is it really possible to be happy with so many things going wrong in one's life?

Yes! When you know how to manage problems effectively, you can enjoy each day of living despite the challenges that your life brings. Here's how to do it:

- Put problem-solving into your schedule. Allow yourself

ten, twenty, or thirty minutes a day to think about one problem. Choose the most urgent one to work on first. During your problem-solving session you can either think things through quietly to yourself, or write down your ideas (you might want to keep a special journal for this purpose), or talk it through with someone (see below). The main point here is that you *only* think about your problem during the time of day you have allotted for it. At all other times of day, you do not allow yourself to think about any problems. You just enjoy whatever's going on that day.

- Work on your problems by
  a) defining them as clearly as possible,
  b) finding realistic solutions that will remove or reduce the problem even a little,
  c) finding thoughts to think that make the problem less severe.
- Each day, take steps to apply one or more of the solutions that you thought of. Keep a written record of your progress if possible or report to your listening friend how you are doing. Don't try to solve a problem all at once — just work on it gradually, doing something about it one day at a time.
- Decide to accept and live with the part of the problem that can't be changed at all (in a few cases, this will be the whole problem, but in most cases it won't be). Remember that everything that happens to you is ultimately for the good[18] even if you don't see the benefits yourself. Hashem has a reason for everything He does, and there is a purpose even in your problem. Trusting that something good will

come out of the problem helps you to live with it.
- Find a person you can talk to about your concerns.[19] Often, we can think things through better when there is someone there to listen. Another person can have valuable insights and ideas, or a completely fresh way of looking at your problem. Also, another person can offer emotional support, which goes a long way toward helping you deal with tough situations. Of course, this person needs to be someone who knows how to listen. It needs to be a person whose wisdom and advice you trust. It needs to be someone who obviously handles his own life well. It may be a friend, a neighbor, a teacher, a counselor, or a rabbi.
- Do not discuss your problems with lots of people. In fact, be careful not to discuss your problems at all outside of their "allotted" time. Do not even repeat your problem over and over to just one person. Say it once, twice at the most, and start to work on solving it. Too much discussion and too little action toward solving problems keeps you in a state of unhappiness. Get on with life.
- Pray. Turning to your Creator for solace and guidance makes sense — and brings relief. Ask Him to help you bear your burden. Maintaining a close personal link with God is the quickest, surest route to peace of mind.

Let's see how this whole process might work with Ruth's problem. Ruth is upset because she's not popular. In the past, she tended to worry about her lack of popularity all day long, feeling awkward on the way to school when others walked down the streets in groups, feeling awkward at school when others mingled and socialized, feeling awkward on the way home as the groups formed again, feeling awkward after school hours as others called each other or got together. In other words, she spent her whole life feeling unhappy about her problem. Now, following the problem-solving model, Ruth does the following:

1) She doesn't permit herself to think about her lack of popularity except during the half-hour before her bedtime. When she walks to school, she focuses on the beauty of the day, or some ideas she has for a project, or something she read about — anything at all other than her relationship to her peers — and she does the same on the way home. While at school, she concentrates on her studies, draws pictures during her free time, and writes out a letter to a relative during her lunch break: she keeps herself occupied and keeps her mind off her "problem."

2) During her half hour problem-solving session, Ruth defines her problem as lacking a close friend and two or three regular "companion" friends. She writes down a few ideas on how she might go about getting closer to people. One of her ideas is to find a book that has information on making and keeping friends. Another idea is to talk to her cousin for advice. Another idea is to join an extra-curricular program where she might meet people from other schools and thereby broaden her base of potential companions.

3) Ruth decides that she should be able to accumulate a couple of companions if she takes the appropriate steps, though she's not sure that she can arrange to have a close friend. She's willing to live without that for the time being. She generates the thought that it's okay to have casual friends even when you're lacking a best friend. She also

works on the thought that her own personal value doesn't depend on how many friends she has.

4) Ruth calls her cousin on Monday and arranges to meet the next week. On Tuesday she goes to the library and looks up a few books dealing with the subject of friendships. On Wednesday, she signs up for group art lessons. On Thursday she starts to read the books she took out of the library.

Each day brings Ruth closer to her goal of acquiring a circle of companions. She no longer mopes about this problem all day long; instead, she allows herself to enjoy every day while thinking of everything other than her problem (except during its allotted time). Simultaneously, Ruth actively works toward solving her problem. By managing her challenge successfully, Ruth has removed a major barrier to her happiness.

Happiness Skill #7:
SET YOUR OWN STANDARDS

Many people make themselves unhappy through their need to win the approval of others. When a person is overly concerned about others' opinion of her, she can't enjoy her own life: she's too busy fearing rejection and ridicule. This can be such a problem that approval-seeking can ruin your life![20]

"The truth is that I'm always worried about what others think of me. Will they like what I'm wearing? Will they think what I've said is clever or dumb? Am I standing the right way? Am I doing the right thing? My worries go on and on. I don't enjoy myself around people because of these thoughts. I just can't relax."

"I'm always worried if people will think my house is too small and plain. Most of my friends live in much fancier places."

"If my group of friends is reading a certain book, I'll read it too, just so I can be in on the conversations — even if I hate the book, I'll read it. I can't tolerate being left out: they might think there's something the matter with me."

"I can't possibly give a public speech. I can't even ask a question or give my opinion when I'm in a group of people — I'm always terrified to open my mouth: will I make a terrible mistake? Will I make a fool of myself? Will people think I'm stupid or inadequate?"

Approval seekers decide that they're "okay" if other people give them approval. If you're an approval seeker, you are leaving your happiness up to others: if they like you, you'll be happy; if they don't, you won't.

An easier way to be happy is to set your own standards. If *you* like your hairstyle, then it's okay. If *you* like your house, then it's grand. If *you* know you are doing the right thing, trying your best, and being yourself, then you are *fine*. If *you* decide that you are at least as capable and smart as the average person, then you can permit yourself to do what other people do and expect to succeed at least as well as others succeed. If *you* give yourself permission to make mistakes and be human, then it'll be okay if you make some mistakes. You set the standards for your success — and if you set them in such a way that you always succeed, then you'll always be happy.

Remember: nobody can please everybody all of the

time. There's no point in trying to. On the other hand, everybody will please some people some of the time. In other words, some people will always like what you're wearing and some won't. Some people will agree with what you are saying and others won't. Some people will like your house and others won't. And who cares if they like it or don't? (In fact, most of the time, people are not even bothering to judge you or your accomplishments — they're too busy wondering how *you* are judging *them*!) The only thing that will make you happy is *your* enjoyment of yourself and your possessions. As long as none of your behavior is wrong, you are entitled to live as you like. And if you like how you live, you'll be happy!

**Happiness Skill #8:
THROW YOURSELF INTO LIFE**

True happiness comes from applying yourself to life in a meaningful way. Wasting one's life in a constant pursuit of fun and stimulation is the path to misery, not to joy. Eventually, a person realizes that superficial excitement is only superficial living: the pleasure of eating an ice-cream cone is over the minute the eating is finished. How many ice-cream cones need one consume to be "happy?" How many new clothes will do the trick? How many trips are necessary?

These pleasure-seeking routes to happiness are actually a desperate attempt to distract oneself from the emptiness of life. People try to pack their days with fun in order to enjoy their lives, yet they find that their lives are not happy. That is because true happiness does not come from having fun — it is the result of doing satisfying, meaningful activities, of fulfilling your purpose in life.

"Organizing the school play was a fantastic experience for me. I had so many responsibilities and it was really hard work, but I grew a lot from the experience. I had to make decisions on my own, I had to delegate tasks and coordinate everything and everybody. I had to see to it that everyone cooperated and got along. It was quite a challenge but it was very satisfying."

"I get a lot of pleasure from helping out with the younger kids in my family. I know my mom really appreciates my help, and the little ones adore me. It's good to feel needed and important."

"I volunteer as a 'big brother' to a little guy whose father died last year. I help him with his homework and I take him places after school. I chat with him on the phone. It gives me a great feeling to be able to help someone like that."

"In my spare time I'm learning to type and sew. These are important skills and I feel pretty accomplished knowing that I can do these things."

Some of the most pleasurable activities in life are helping other people and learning new things. The more you immerse yourself in truly significant activities, the more happiness you will have. Imagine the satisfaction that comes, for example, from calling up someone who you know is probably lonely. If you have five spare minutes, try doing just that and see how it feels. The feeling that you will experience will not be called "fun." Yet, the glow from it will last many hours and days beyond the moment of the phone call. This feeling comes from the true satisfaction that creates a life of happiness.

In fact, you can structure your free time to include many activities that will contribute to your growth as a human being and consequently contribute to your happiness. Don't waste opportunities for real happiness by "doing nothing" or just reading novels. Instead, try volunteering your services where they are needed, increase your learning, bake cakes for your mother or others, write letters to people who will be thrilled to hear from you, write a book, talk to a friend who needs someone to listen, draw pictures for the children in your life — anything you do that brings a smile to others boomerangs into joy and happiness for yourself. Throw yourself into life — don't be a passive bystander! Make your happiness happen!

These happiness skills will get you started on a lifetime habit of happiness. Use them and enjoy!

6
Caring: The Key to Success

CARING — FOR YOURSELF and others — is the key to a successful life. Caring for yourself means appreciating the person you are and treating yourself with respect. Caring for others means appreciating them and treating them with respect.

When kindness and caring permeate your interactions with the world, yours will be a life of peace, happiness, and true success.

Question:

> "How can I care for others when they don't treat me properly? How can I treat someone with kindness, for example, when he constantly hurts my feelings?"

Answer:

> That's a good question. In most cases, people who hurt the feelings of others are basically good people

who are making a bad mistake. Focus on the good parts of that person when you are interacting with him. Remind yourself of his positive qualities — really think about them and picture them. By doing so, you'll be able to treat him nicely. Your nice treatment will discourage him from continuing to be unkind to you. This takes time, but eventually you will notice a change in him. It's worth waiting for, so don't give up! (P.S. This works on family members as well as other people.)

Question:

"How can caring be the key to success? What if you're a caring person but everything in your life goes wrong: you fail in school, can't get a good job, can't find a marriage partner, can't afford to dress well — one disaster after another. Can you really have a successful life just because you 'care'?"

Answer:

When you care about yourself, you'll always be a success. Caring about yourself means that you value yourself as a human being. You understand that your life has a purpose and that all of your "obstacles" to success are no more than challenges sent to you to help you attain that purpose. Rising to those challenges is what constitutes your success. Always give yourself encouragement and love; don't kick yourself (that's not caring!) because this only weakens you, destroying your ability to handle whatever comes your way. Rather, trust yourself to succeed; praise yourself for your efforts; comfort and console yourself by keeping close to your Creator. Yes, care about yourself, and you will be successful!

Question:

"I've tried everything in my desire to find happiness. There were times when I was really caring toward my family, but since nobody noticed or appreciated my efforts, I gave up. There were times when I worked on self-improvement programs for myself, but they never lasted long. I really wonder if I'll ever be happy. How much should a person try before giving up and becoming resigned to a life of unhappiness?"

Answer:

It's great to hear that you are a person who tries. Someone who doesn't try has no chance of living a successful life! In fact, if you do want to find happiness, you will have to look for it EVERY DAY. You will have to TRY every day to bring happiness into your life, because this is not something that arrives one day and stays from then on. On the contrary, happiness comes every day that you put forth the effort to bring it into your life. If you want a good day, you must decide first thing in the morning that you will make it a good day and then you must work the whole day through to see that it is! People who make each day happy, one day at a time, will have happy lives. So keep up with your efforts and never give up. That's the path to success.

Question:

"I really like the ideas you've presented — they all make a lot of sense and I must say I've learned a few new things. Although I benefitted from reading the book, I have a friend who I feel could REALLY benefit from reading it. She is quite down in the dumps about herself and her situation. I'd like her to learn some of the concepts and skills you've taught here, but I don't know how to expose her to them. Should I just hand her the book or would that give her the impression that I think she needs help?"

Answer:

If you know someone who could benefit from this book, the best way to get them to read it is to share your enthusiasm with them. Just tell them about a great book that you read; tell them why you found it interesting. This won't make anyone defensive — on the contrary, it will spark their interest and make them eager to read it for themselves.

Question:

"I think of myself as a caring person, but for some reason I have a lot of trouble making and keeping friends. I end up feeling isolated and alone most of the time. How am I supposed to be able to be successful and happy when I feel this way?"

Answer:

Even good, caring people can have trouble acquiring friends. By lowering your standards somewhat (i.e., settling for being with people who aren't exactly your type), you'd probably be able to make some "companionship" friends to do things with so that you won't feel so lonely. However, nothing really removes the pain of not having an intimate friend except acquiring an intimate friend — something which isn't always possible. Despite this loss, you can certainly be a happy, fulfilled person providing you direct your energies in a meaningful way. Remember to stay active and involved in life: don't wait for a friend to come and "make" your life fulfilled — start fulfilling your own life today. Give of yourself to others (family and community) and by doing this, your "hole" will be speedily filled.

Question:

"I'm really looking forward to getting married, building my own home, and having a great life. I know that once I leave my parents' home, where there are a lot of tensions, everything is going to be fine. Isn't it true that a good marriage with a loving partner can heal all the wounds of your past and guarantee a life of happiness and success?"

Answer:

A good marriage can definitely enhance the happiness of one's adult life. But how does one get a good marriage? It's not from marrying a "good" person! The majority of people are "good" in their own right, but the ability to make a relationship work depends on having and using the kinds of skills that are illustrated in *Teen Esteem*. Success and happiness are never handed to us on a silver platter; they are prizes that we must work toward ourselves. You and your marriage partner can attain them by caring about each other and caring about yourselves in the ways that we have discussed in this book.

Question:

"You make it seem like life is one big problem! Why does everything take so much work? Why do you paint such a gloomy picture of challenges and difficulties that must be overcome? Doesn't anyone have a simple life of contentment? I, myself, am a happy person from a happy home and I expect to have a happy life without a bunch of problems! And I had all this before I read your book!"

Answer:

That's terrific! You and your family are obviously doing a lot of things right. To you, it seems perfectly natural to be happy and content with life. No obvious impediments to happiness have blocked your path. Without even realizing it, you have developed a set of Positive Power tapes that give you a bright and optimistic outlook on life. *Teen Esteem* strives to give everyone the benefit of a positive attitude and great coping skills. It's true that some people don't have many major "problems" to deal with in their lives and that may give them a head start on living happily. However, happy, successful living is possible even when there are problems to be dealt with.

Moreover, "problems" do not necessarily refer to traumatic difficulties such as death, divorce, illness, and so on. Rather, a "problem" is anything, no matter how minor, that a person must deal with — such as having tests at school, learning a new skill, negotiating an argument with a friend, or deciding what to do in one's free time. And life is filled with those kinds of "problems" for everyone, but lucky people like yourself don't perceive these challenges as problems at all. To you, they are just the everyday issues of living. And really, that is how it should be for everyone. Reading *Teen Esteem* will give others the same comfortable perception that you already have. They, too, will be able to view life as a simple and happy affair without obvious difficulties.

Question:

"Is that all there is then? After reading *Teen Esteem*, will I know everything there is about how to live a successful life?"

Answer:

Well, not quite! Living a successful and happy life is a constant and lifelong challenge. The issues change at every stage of life. There is so much to learn. *Teen*

Esteem is a starting point really. With the proper skills and outlook, you can continue the process of growth, continue to reach out and learn, continue to apply yourself to life and thereby reach your potential in every way. Delve into the wisdom of our Torah; learn from our Sages. Herein lie the secrets to a life of true peace and contentment — a life of true success.

Notes

Chapter One

1. *Mesillas Yesharim*, ch. 1.
2. *Sanhedrin* 37a.
3. Vayikra 19:15.
4. Zelig Pliskin, *Gateway To Happiness* (New York: Jewish Learning Exchange, 1983), p. 231.
5. Shemos 23:7; Vayikra 25:24; *Bava Metzia* 58b.
6. Mordechai Menachem Reich, *Torah: The Crown of Wisdom* (Lakewood, N.J.: Halacha Publications, 1983), intro.
7. Devarim 30:19.
8. *Niddah* 16b.
9. Vayikra 19:18.
10. Ibid.
11. Koheles 3:1-8.
12. *Alei Shor*, vol. 1, ch. 5.
13. *Taanis* 22a.

Chapter Two

1. *Chayei Adam* 67:3.
2. One who properly honors and reveres his parents is promised

"long life" both in this world and the World to Come (*Yoreh Deah* 240:1).
3. Vayikra 19:15.
4. Mishlei 29:17.
5. Rambam, *Hilchos De'os* 6:7-8.
6. Devarim 27:16; Rambam, *Hilchos De'os* 6:7.
7. *Yoreh Deah* 240:11.
8. Ibid. 240:2.
9. Ibid.
10. Mishlei 10:1.
11. *Menoras HaMaor.*
12. Mishlei 13:24.
13. Vayikra 25:17.
14. *Biur HaGra* 240:36; *Teshuvos Rabbi Akiva Eiger* 68.
15. *Iggeres HaRamban.*
16. *Yoreh Deah* 240:2.
17. Ibid. 240:11.

Chapter Three

1. *Yoreh Deah* 240:22.
2. Vayikra 19:18.
3. Ibid. 25:17.
4. *Nedarim* 22a.
5. Vayikra 25:17.
6. *Sanhedrin* 102b.
7. *Bava Metzia* 58b.
8. *Tamid* 28a; *Pirkei Avos* 6:6; *Derech Eretz Zuta* 9.
9. Tehillim 34:15.
10. *Berachos* 17a; *Avos deRabbi Nasan* 28:3.
11. *Shemos Rabbah* 30.
12. *Pirkei Avos* 4:1.
13. Vayikra 25:17.
14. *Chafetz Chayim, Ahavas Chessed*, part 2, ch. 22.
15. Shemos 22:13.
16. *Choshen Mishpat* 358:1.

17. *Yoreh Deah* 334:123.
18. *Pesachim* 112a.
19. *Sanhedrin* 7a.
20. Vayikra 19:18.
21. Ibid. 19:17.
22. Rambam, *Hilchos De'os* 7:7.

Chapter Four

1. *Taanis* 23a.
2. Shmuel Yerushalmi, *MeAm Lo'ez: The Book of Koheleth* (Jerusalem: Moznaim Publishing Corporation, 1986), p. 104.
3. Samson Raphael Hirsch, *From the Wisdom of Mishlei*, (Jerusalem: Feldheim Publishers, 1976), p. 184.
4. Mishlei 27:17.
5. Hirsch, *From the Wisdom of Mishlei.*
6. *Midrash Rabbah.*
7. *Pirkei Avos* 3:12.
8. *Derech Eretz Zuta* 2.
9. *Pirkei Avos* 6:5.
10. *Yoma* 75a.
11. Vayikra 25:17.
12. Ibid. 19:18.
13. Koheles 9:17.
14. *Berachos* 17a.
15. Zelig Pliskin, *Gateway To Happiness* (New York: Jewish Learning Exchange, 1983), p. 57.
16. Mishlei 17:17.
17. Rav Chaim Shmuelevitz, cited by Zelig Pliskin, *Love Your Neighbor* (Aish HaTorah Publications, 1977), p. 310.
18. Shemos 23:7.
19. Vayikra 25:17.
20. *Pirkei Avos* 2:3.
21. Mishlei 13:20.
22. *Sefer Chassidim.*
23. *Divrei Chassidim.*

24. Mordechai Menachem Reich, *Torah: The Crown of Wisdom* (Lakewood N.J.: Halacha Publications, 1983), on *Mishlei* 25:17.
25. *Pirkei Avos* 3:12.

Chapter Five

1. *Mishlei* 17:22; *Tehillim* 687:4.
2. *Chovos HaLevavos* 10:7.
3. *Chochmah U'Mussar*, vol. 2, p. 74.
4. *Koheles Rabbasi* 1:34.
5. *Pirkei Avos* 4:1.
6. *Sefer HaChinuch*, mitzvah 16.
7. *Sanhedrin* 100b.
8. *Chochmah U'Mussar*, vol. 2, pg. 331-2.
9. Ibid. p. 24.
10. *Sanhedrin* 102b; *Kiddushin* 40b; *Iyov* 5:2; *Pesachim* 113b.
11. *Mesillas Yesharim*, ch. 22.
12. *Chayei HaMussar*, vol. 1, p. 107.
13. *Vayikra* 25:17.
14. *Chochmah U'Mussar*, vol. 2, p. 218.
15. *Iggeres HaRamban*.
16. *Vayikra* 19:15.
17. Zelig Pliskin, *Gateway To Happines* (New York: Jewish Learning Exchange, 1983), p. 209.
18. *Chochmah U'Mussar*, vol. 2, p. 24.
19. *Yoma* 75a.
20. *Pirkei Avos* 4:28.